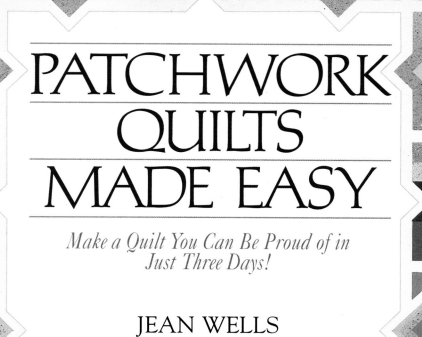

PATCHWORK QUILTS MADE EASY

*Make a Quilt You Can Be Proud of in
Just Three Days!*

JEAN WELLS

C&T PUBLISHING

Rodale Press
Emmaus, Pennsylvania

OUR MISSION

We publish books that empower people's lives.

RODALE BOOKS

Printed in the United States of America on acid-free ∞ recycled paper ♲, containing 10 percent post-consumer waste.

Photography: Ross Chandler
Illustrations: Dennis McGregor, Ginny Coull, and Micaela Carr
Design and Production Coordinator: Irene Morris, Morris Design

C&T Publishing Staff
Managing Editor: Liz Aneloski
Copy Editor: Louise Owens Townsend
Technical Editor: Dalene Young Stone
Art Production Editor: Diane Pedersen
Photo Editor: Florence Stone
Illustration Editor:
  Barbara Konzak Kuhn

Rodale Press Staff
Executive Editor: Margaret Lydic Balitas
Managing Editor: Suzanne Nelson
Associate Editor: Ellen Pahl
Assistant Editor: Karen Costello Soltys
Copy Editor: Maria Zator
Cover Designer: Darlene Schneck
Cover Photographer: Mitch Mandel
Cover Stylist: Dee Schlagel,
  Design Discovery

If you have any questions or comments concerning this book, please write to:

Rodale Press
Book Readers' Service
33 East Minor Street
Emmaus, PA 18098

A pattern for the cover quilt *Autumn Pines* appears on page 183. The Amish bed bench was loaned courtesy of Louise H. Strauz, Strauz Antiques, 2083 Main Street, Churchtown, PA 17555. The cover was photographed at Glasbern Inn, an inn in the country, RD#1 Box 250, Fogelsville, PA 18051.

Library of Congress Cataloging-in-Publication Data
Wells-Keenan, Jean
    Patchwork quilts made easy : make a quilt you can be proud of in just three days / Jean Wells
        p. cm.
    ISBN 0-87596-628-4 (hardcover)
    1. Patchwork quilts. 2. Patchwork—Patterns. 3. Machine sewing. I. Title
TT835.K44   1994
746.9'7—dc20   94-16959
                                    CIP

Distributed in the book trade by St. Martin's Press

Distributed in the quilt/sewing trade by C&T Publishing

2 4 6 8 10 9 7 5 3 1   hardcover

DEDICATION

To Ursula Searles, my friend, my creative helper, a precision piecer who continues to be an inspiration to all quilters she meets.

TABLE OF CONTENTS

PREFACE

Patchwork Quilts Made Easy is just that! So many quilt designs appear complicated, but they really aren't when you become familiar with them. I will introduce you to a world full of color and design in quilting. You will see your confidence soar as you learn the easy, time-saving cutting and stitching techniques that make quiltmaking so rewarding. This text is filled with "easy" step-by-step instructions and charts to make your quilting journey a successful one.

As I worked on Patchwork Quilts Made Easy, it took me back to my beginnings in quiltmaking. My first quilt was finished while awaiting the arrival of my now 25-year-old son. My actual sewing career began at 9 years old, making doll clothing. A home economics degree was earned in college, followed by a teaching career that has developed into a much more extensive career of owning a quilt shop for 20 years and writing how-to quilting books.

In my 25 years as a quiltmaker and quilt-shop owner, I have worked with a large number of students and customers. The never-ending array of projects that I see and help move to the final stages is marvelous. My goal has always been to help the student and customer through efficient and creative methods of decision making so they can be successful on their own.

Writing books is a teaching tool for me. Pretend you are in one of my classes. For the new quiltmaker, you will learn techniques for cutting and sewing that assure accuracy and a quilt to be proud of.

For the experienced quilter, you will find design and color inspiration as well as a chance to brush up on techniques. In the Color Awareness section, I have taken you through the discussion that I use with my beginning students, making you aware of the decisions that you will be making. Complete instructions are included in Chapter 2 on constructing and finishing a quilt.

Each chapter contains an introduction to the specific style of quilts in that chapter. Next come the block construction techniques. The quilts that follow are a variation on that theme with complete start-to-finish directions. Instructions are "quilter friendly" with square symbols that are color-coded to help you with fabric identification. I designed three sampler quilts for the final chapter, each of which uses several different blocks from the rest of the book. You can start here if you are interested in trying a variety of blocks.

Color, design, and construction insights are sprinkled throughout the text in decorative boxes to alert you to an idea or an inspiration. I hope from your Patchwork Quilts Made Easy experience that you will develop a love of creating color and pattern that goes with quiltmaking. When you work on a quilt, you are making something worthwhile, whether it is to keep someone warm, adorn a wall, or accessorize a room. Enjoy!

LEFT TO RIGHT:

Sawtooth Trail begins on page 75.

Starry Pinwheels begins on page 62.

Primarily Stars begins on page 80.

COME TO SISTERS

Creativity and

uniqueness dwell

in this small

mountain community

where Jean Wells

lives and works.

She has chosen settings near her Oregon home

for the quilts in Patchwork Quilts Made Easy

that showcase them in inspirational locations.

A creek runs through the quaint shop-filled town that is surrounded by ponderosa pines and the spectacular Cascade Mountains. Each summer, a beautiful array of locally made quilts spreads out across the fronts of shops and homes in the largest outdoor quilt show in America.

(Hanging at left) Basket Trellis begins on page 158. (On left-hand bench) Garden Variety begins on page 117, and Bloomin' Bear's Paw begins on page 196.

(Hanging left of doorway) Checkerboard Bunnies begins on page 111. (Hanging from balcony) Tessellating Stars begins on page 97.

(Hanging right of doorway) Sawtooth Garden begins on page 77. (On right-hand bench) Hour Glass Pinwheels begins on page 68, and Emily's Cottage begins on page 218.

(Hanging at right) Bow Tie Fans begins on page 140.

Gone Fishing begins on page 249.

Pinebrook begins on page 215.

Enjoy the beauty of these easy-to-make quilts in their timeless settings while you collect color ideas from both the quilts and their surroundings.

Bunny Hop begins on page 108.

1930s Log Cabin begins on page 179.

CHAPTER ONE

Color Awareness

When you look at a quilt, color is what you notice first, before design and before workmanship. Color sets the mood in a quilt. Vivid color combinations can grab you and pull you toward them: Subtle combinations calm you, and rich, earthy combinations like the *Autumn Pines* quilt on the cover are warm and inviting. Color can excite a variety of reactions in us. Choosing colors for a quilt is a major aspect of the quiltmaking process.

All people have an intuitive color sense but don't always realize it. Most people just lack confidence. Color speaks directly to us. We either like it or we don't. Colors evoke a reaction or a response. They have power! Our personal experiences that are locked in our memories play a big part in our reaction to color. Having owned my own quilt shop for 20 years and taught quilting for 25 years, I've worked with thousands of people making color decisions for quilting projects. We all have definite opinions about what we like and don't like. Begin with your own response to color but be open to expanding your ideas and gaining color sensitivity.

Choosing colors is an observation process. In addition to looking at quilts and learning from other quilters' tastes, become an observer. Notice your own surroundings. Look closely at the pansies in early spring. See how nature deals with colors so naturally within a single flower. A pansy might be mostly deep purple with a small amount of intense yellow in the center or just the opposite. You can transfer this to a quilt design by using 80% shades and tints of purple and 20% yellow. The proportions of the colors will be pleasing. If it works in a flower, it will work in a quilt!

Pansy-inspired Palette

This "proportion rule" is a good one to follow yourself. For example, if you have chosen a dusty blue and old rose combination for a Log Cabin quilt, you might make the blocks half rose and half blue. They are 50% of each color. As you take a look at them, your eye will be confused. This is because it can't decide if it is a blue quilt or a rose quilt. If you choose a rose border, the quilt becomes more rose, and you won't be confused when you look at it.

Use this rule when you choose colors for a quilt: Make it shades and tints of mostly one color and then pull in a second color for interest. A third color can be added that is a lot brighter or darker—one that is of higher contrast to accent the other colors in a combination. The quilt on the cover has a small amount of purple in it, and the purple just makes it sing. Sometimes I use the accent in a thin border as I did in the *Garden Variety* bunny quilt on page 117. It brings the colors to life.

Be aware of your neighborhood. Look at buildings, houses, landscaping, or sunsets to gain color clues to use later. Thousands of dollars are spent on advertisements so save magazine ads that have color combinations that inspire you. Greeting cards, seed catalogs, decorating magazines, and wallpaper books all have ideas waiting for you.

Look to nature to discover color beginnings. Everyone can relate to nature. Green is the color of grass; it is calming. Blue is a sky color; it is expansive and lights up a setting. Red is nature's bright spot. Think about poppies or raspberries. Yellow is like the morning sun. It is bright and cheery—it is a new beginning. Purple is rich.

I live in a rural area and enjoy gardening, so flowers and trees are a source of ideas for me as are the colors I see reflected on the mountains nearby. Color in nature changes with the time of day and season of the year. The reflection of morning sun on clean winter snow is vivid pink and purple, while in the late spring those colors are a duller pinky-peach and mauve because the snow is dirty. *Train yourself to be an observer,* and collect color ideas in your mind to pull out and use later.

Color schemes have to start somewhere. Quilt shows, quilt books, and magazines are full of quilts others have created. Learn from these quilts. Think about what you are seeing. Observe how the maker has combined colors and fabrics. Train yourself to analyze what you like and don't like, what works and doesn't work. In this process, you will develop your own intuitive color sense. Always remember that this is an ongoing process. You will build concepts and in the process refine earlier ones in order to grow.

I keep a file folder of ideas, whether it be an ad from a magazine, a greeting card, a snapshot from a quilt show, a swatch of fabric, or a painting by a child. When I need inspiration, I look through these ideas, and usually something grabs me.

As you study color and its use, you will find your tastes turn to certain color families—maybe it is a season of the year like fall or a time of the day like the early morning misty colors or a variety of blues that excite you.

Remember that color is a way you will express your creativity. Color sense is in all of us. It can be brought to life and encouraged to blossom through experience, awareness, and study. Become a student of color, and a whole world will open up to you.

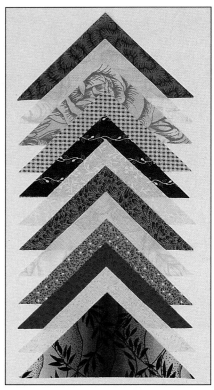

Nature's blues and greens coupled with the pinks and reds of poppies are interspersed with neutrals for this scrap quilt palette.

PROPERTIES OF COLOR

Let's look at some color basics that will help you to define your ideas and make color decisions.

Value is the lightness or darkness of a color. A color becomes lighter if you add white and darker if you add black. The *contrast* of light, medium, and dark fabrics in a quilt will help define the shapes in the quilt design. Look at the *Galaxy* quilt on page 94. The star shapes are very defined in the blue and white combination. In the *Star Gardens* quilt on page 92, the fabrics don't have as high a contrast level so there is less definition.

If you are uncertain whether you have enough *contrast* in your fabric choices, cut a small swatch of each and put them in a copy machine. This reduces them to black, white, and gray. You will immediately know which fabric is lighter and which is darker. Even though you might have a red and blue fabric, which are two different colors, they might be the same *value*.

How this translates into quilting is that when you look at the quilt from a distance, the red and blue will mix together, and the individual shapes of the pieces will be less defined.

What I do when I'm working at home is to put the fabrics up on a piece of white flannel or dense batting that has been pinned or taped to a wall.

Then I walk to the other side of the room and turn around and quickly glance at them. An impression will be left in my mind. Trust that impression! If your colors run together and look boring, make a change. If one fabric jumps out at you and looks like a sore thumb, change it.

I find I can also walk across the room and squint at the fabrics and this reduces them to their value. There are inexpensive reducing glasses (which look like a magnifying glass) available at most quilt shops. When held up to a quilt block, the glass will reduce the block as a photograph does, and you can easily see the contrast. First impressions do work. If a combination is not working on the wall, it probably won't work in the quilt.

Contrast is the property that will make the quilt design interesting. It helps to define shapes in the design that will create patterns; it is the difference between light and dark. You must have contrast between the main pattern and the background pieces in order to see the design—for example, pieced stars must have contrast between the stars and the background in order to see the stars. The contrast in the quilt is emphasized by the sparkle—a small amount of brighter, lighter, or darker fabric that makes the others work together. The yellow stars add sparkle to *Primarily Stars* on page 80, and really make the quilt sing.

Intensity is the amount of saturation in a color. Think of true red compared to a red that has white added to it. The true red is richer. Sometimes another color is added to a true color to create a full-bodied effect, like a little blue added to a red to create magenta. It certainly is more intense than true red. The intense colors will jump out at you in a design or appear bolder and larger. Mostly I use them for an accent in a quilt design to enhance another combination. In the *Mountain Sunrise* quilt on page 186, the rich magenta makes the blues and teals pop. Without it, the quilt looks dull.

Color temperature in a palette affects us emotionally. Yellows are bright and intense, as warm as sunshine or as cool as lemon sherbet. Blues will be warm if they contain some green and cooler if they contain white or some violet.

Warmer and lighter colors will advance toward you, and the spaces they fill will appear larger. Cooler and darker colors will recede into the background and appear smaller. When you combine fabrics in a quilt, the temperature the fabric radiates affects the colors around it. The contrast you choose to work with might be a warm-cool contrast instead of a light-dark one.

Primarily Stars on page 80 is a good example of how warm colors advance. The gold and red stars come at you and pop while the blue stars tend to recede. The green is an olive green that has some yellow in it. It becomes almost neutral and doesn't advance or recede. The black background fabric is a quiet background for all of the star movement. The difference between warm and cool also can be contrast.

FABRIC SELECTION

Not only are you dealing with color when you go to choose fabrics for a quilt, you are dealing with pattern and style. You have thousands of fabrics from which to choose. The *mood* or *style* of a fabric is important to the design of the quilt. Some florals come across very frilly and create a Victorian or feminine mood while others in rich, dark colors might be more elegant in their appearance. Fabric can be cute, contemporary, elegant, country, sophisticated, whimsical, subtly textured, and so forth. Stripes and plaids lend a country feeling or geometric mood to a fabric combination. Tiny floral "calicoes" will look very traditional. The color and design of the fabric will contribute to its mood.

Scale refers to the size of the design in a print. To create more interest, vary the scale of the design in your fabric choices. For example, you might have a large floral, small stripe or plaid, and a medium textured leaf all in one quilt. You will see a large variety in scale of prints in the palette in the photos here.

Visual texture is how a fabric appears from a distance. There are many fabrics available now that I call "textured solids." They are two-color designs that are low contrast. When viewed from a distance, they appear as a texture. They are "blenders." They help to make a higher contrast print work. They are not bold like a solid color is.

Prints will have an impact on the quilt visually. They create movement. Be sure to consider the impact when you are planning a quilt. Observe the print. Is it a textured solid that you will read as a subtle texture from a distance or does it have bold contrast like a stripe?

Florals can be packed tightly together where hardly any background shows or they might appear viney or in clusters where the background shows. Large florals offer a variety of cutting options to the creative quilter.

Fabrics come in many different styles: feminine or Victorian, whimsical, elegant, traditional calico, textured solid, and contemporary.

Using a Window Template

Think about your template shape in a block design. Cut out a window in a piece of paper the size of the template. This window can be moved around on the print to show you different cutting options.

Swirling geometrics will add movement in the quilt design. Printed checks add a whimsical look. See *Donna's Sampler* on page 238. Large dots will always appear as spots in a quilt design. Solids work well in quilts where you want definition or a rest. They appear more dramatic and are quiet at the same time. I like nothing better than a quilt made of all solids like the *Twilight Bear's Paw* quilt on page 202. This is a great example of creating sharp, clear images.

PUTTING IT ALL TOGETHER

My favorite parts of quilting are picking the fabric and planning the design. Sometimes I collect fabric for a quilt that I have in mind for a long time. It's fun to pick up a little piece here and there. The gathering becomes part of the story that the quilt has to tell.

As you make plans for a quilt, pull any fabrics that you have at home before you set out for the quilt shop or fabric store. Be prepared with an idea in mind but always be flexible. You don't know what wonderful fabric you might find that will change the look of your quilt for the better. Always remember that you know what you like and don't like—you have a natural, intuitive color sense that you are further developing through quilting.

If you don't have a "theme" fabric, pick one. A theme fabric is one that sets the mood and color of your quilt. Remember that fabric designers are talented, artistic people who can help you develop your ideas. Observe what the designer has done in terms of color combinations as well as the percentage she has used of each color. If it is mostly shades of blue with some pink and yellow and green, take your cue from that and choose fabrics in that same proportion. Vary the scale and design of the prints to make it interesting. Choose a "sparkle," an accent fabric that makes the others sing. Sometimes it means using a small amount of a brighter or lighter or darker shade of something.

Remember when you are choosing these fabrics that you are seeing the whole bolt but that in your quilt one of these might be used in a smaller amount. The accent might only be 5% of the design. Turn the bolt so that a smaller amount of the fabric shows. This will make a huge difference when you view the fabrics from a distance. This shows proportion. It puts them in perspective. Step away from the fabrics, walk a few steps, turn around and get a first impression. Do you need to make adjustments? If you have adjusted the amounts of the fabrics showing to reflect the quilt design, maybe a fabric needs to be replaced if it isn't working.

Many times the theme fabric will end up only being the inspiration for choosing the palette and not appear in the quilt, or it may become the border or backing.

Many fabric companies design groups of fabrics that coordinate with each other. Usually there is a theme fabric with coordinates or extractions (smaller prints taken from the theme idea). Your job is made easier if you just pick a whole group, but sometimes it is just too predictable. It will be more interesting if you toss in fabrics from other manufacturers. Add a plaid or a textured solid or a more vivid accent. The *Gone Fishing* quilt on page 249 is a good example. The fish fabrics are from one company but other prints with interesting visual texture complement the palette, and red is the accent.

Don't overmatch your fabrics. I can remember when I first started my store and people would try to match a tiny ⅛" rosebud in a print. What happens, especially in smaller prints, is that when you get a distance away, the colors blend and the tiny rosebud will not always appear that same pink. Or a really intense color will look like a bright spot. Pick fabrics that have a similar color mood, and the quilt will be more interesting.

Planning a Palette—pick a theme fabric and use it to choose the other fabrics.

When I choose a palette of fabrics for a quilt, I make sure they have something in common. Maybe it is the festive mood of *Christmas Village* on page 221. I tell my students that the fabrics are like friends.

They are all individuals but they have something in common, and there is always that one that stands out or is a little different, the sparkle. Leaf through this book now just thinking about color planning. Identify what you like and don't like.

REPETITION IN QUILT DESIGN

My favorite class to teach is the sampler class. I think it is a challenge in that you are not working with the same blocks over and over. But the ultimate goal is to create "unity" within the quilt design. This means that you find other things to repeat instead of the quilt block. It might be that any block that has a definite background area is always light or always dark—whatever you choose to keep constant. As you make one block and like two colors together, repeat them together in another block.

The mood of the colors in the little chair was the inspiration for the Watermelon Slices quilt on page 149.

Other "constants" you might consider would be to make all star points dark, or to always use the theme fabric in each block. This develops a repetition that is subtle and will unify the quilt design. You will find things to repeat in the quilt design. When borders are added, they can repeat the bright spot in a print as a solid.

PLANNING BORDERS

The addition of borders to a quilt will frame the design and unify it. When I am designing a quilt, I find it difficult to determine the border until I finish the piecing. I like to look at the pieced top and say to myself, "What does the quilt need?" Please the quilt first, and it will please you and its surroundings. Does it need a border? Should the border be a single fabric or would the addition of two or three fabrics repeated from colors in the quilt work? Look at the different quilts in this book for border ideas.

A border rule that always works for me is to first use a narrow piece of the brightest or darkest color. It will accent the interior. Then follow with a wider border that suggests the main mood of the quilt. If several borders are used, start with the narrowest and cut them wider as you move out. Make sure the border acts as a frame and doesn't detract from the quilt design. It will be a frame for what is happening in the center of the quilt.

CONCLUSION

Look through the designs in this book for fabric, color, and design ideas. Use the book for inspiration. If you like a particular design and want to make that quilt, think about where the darks, lights, and brights have been used. Adjust your fabric choices to reflect this scheme, and your fabrics will work in the quilt design. In this process you will start to say to yourself, "I would have done this or changed that." Congratulations! You are starting to develop your own color and design sense. That is what this quilting process is all about. Have fun!

CHAPTER TWO

Quilting Basics

What Is a Quilt?

A quilt contains three layers—like a sandwich with a fancy top. The top can be patchwork (smaller pieces of different fabrics sewn together) or it might be appliqué (the application of a shape onto a surface), or it might be a combination of both. The middle layer is batting— a non-woven filler material usually made of polyester and sometimes of cotton. The backing is a layer of fabric under the batting. Quilting is the process of stitching the three layers together so the batting doesn't move around. It may be done by hand or by sewing machine.

FABRIC

Fabric has several properties that you must be conscious of while quiltmaking. The selvage edges are tightly woven and run parallel to the lengthwise or straight of grain. The lengthwise threads are strong and have very little give to them. The crosswise grain runs from selvage to selvage. These threads are more flexible when you pull them. The bias runs at a 45° angle across the crosswise and lengthwise grain. It has the most give. Binding that needs to curve should be cut on the bias.

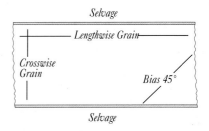

FABRIC PREPARATION

You will have an easier time piecing the top of the quilt if the fabrics are 100% cotton. Cotton is more flexible and has a soft, comfortable hand or feel to it. It takes a press well. Choose fabrics that are tightly woven and of the same weight. A broadcloth weight is most commonly used in quiltmaking.

PURCHASING FABRIC

The projects in this book allow for enough yardage for the project described but not a lot of extra. Sometimes there will be extra from the backing when it has to be pieced.

If you enjoy quilting you will soon be collecting fabrics for future quilts. Part of the quilting process is building the palette. When I am unsure what use the fabric will have, I buy in smaller amounts like "fat quarters" (fabrics that have been cut in 18" x 22" pieces). They work great in scrap quilts or smaller projects. If I absolutely love the fabric and think I might want it for a border, I buy three yards. Otherwise, if it's a fabric I like, I buy in ¾-yard increments.

THE MOOD OF THE QUILT

The first thing that I do when I'm ready to make a quilt is to set some parameters. I ask myself, who is the quilt for? Where will it be used? As soon as these questions are answered, I look for a fabric that sets the mood. This is the theme fabric. It might be a bold geometric, a soft pastel, or a cheerful plaid. From this fabric, start looking for friends—fabrics that have something in common with the theme. By answering the above questions, you narrow down your options and begin to focus in on the project.

If you are unsure whether a fabric will change size or lose color, wash and dry it as you would in a finished project. Warm water and detergent are recommended. Darker fabrics like purples, deep blues, and reds will sometimes lose dye and bleed. If the fabrics you have prewashed are still bleeding, don't use them in a quilt. Before I purchase a fabric, I rub it between my fingers. If the dye comes off, I know it will bleed.

> ❖ *Jill Coe, one of my Sampler class students, came up with the idea of stitching two 1" x 2" strips of fabric together, one a white and one a deep color. Then put them in water. You will soon see if the darker fabric bleeds.*

Most fabrics have some kind of finish that reduces wrinkling. This finish usually doesn't wash out completely. Ones that are really stiff probably will not unstiffen when washed.

QUILTING TOOLS YOU WILL NEED

❖ **Rotary Cutter:** A round, very sharp blade is mounted on a plastic handle. It looks like a pizza cutter. They come in two sizes, small and large. I find the larger cutter easier to handle.

❖ **Cutting Mat**: This is made of plastic; it is self-healing and comes in various sizes. It protects the table during cutting. The 18" x 24" size is ample.

❖ **Rotary Cutting Ruler:** This ⅛"-thick, acrylic see-thru ruler is designed for quilters. It is marked in 1", ½", ¼", and ⅛" increments. A 6" x 12" ruler works well for the projects in this book.

❖ **Fabric Shears:** Sharp fabric-cutting scissors

❖ **Paper-Cutting Scissors**

❖ **Straight Pins:** The finer pins with glass heads will be easiest to see and manipulate, rather than the thick shank pins. Do not sew over pins because distortion will occur in the seam line. Stitch up to them, pull them out, then continue.

❖ **Seam Ripper**

❖ **Tape Measure**

❖ **Iron**

Tools of the Trade

❖ **Sewing Machine:** Be sure it is in good working order.

❖ **Sewing Thread:** A cotton thread is best for piecing when you work with cotton fabrics. Match the thread to the basic mood of the quilt. For most quilts, I use a dull tan. If the quilt is very dark or very light, change the thread color to match. For appliqué, match the thread color to the appliqué fabric.

❖ **Monofilament Thread:** This looks like a clear, thin fishing line. It is often called invisible thread. It is used in the top of your machine when machine quilting. Use a cotton bobbin thread that matches the back of the quilt.

❖ **Quilting Thread:** This is used for hand quilting and is a bit stronger than sewing thread. Traditionally, white or cream-colored thread was used, but there are many other colors available today that can add texture and interest to your project.

> ❖ *Purchase good-quality supplies. They will last longer. It is worth it to invest in quality tools that will help you in being accurate.*

❖ **Needles:** Machine needles for piecing quilts are sized 10 to 14 or 70 to 90. The higher the number, the larger the needle. For cotton fabrics, an average-size needle is recommended. Change the needle with every major project since they get burrs on the side. In hand-sewing projects, a #11 sharp needle works well for sewing and appliqué. Betweens are used for hand quilting. A size 8, 9, or 10 will be the easiest to use. Unlike machine needles, the higher the number, the smaller the needle.

❖ **Needle Threader:** Purchase the one with a different size on each end. Great for threading the tiny quilting needles or fine appliqué needles.

❖ **Beeswax:** This can be rubbed along the thread while hand quilting to make the thread stronger and reduce tangling.

❖ **Thimble:** Be sure it fits the second finger of your stitching hand comfortably.

❖ **Medium-Size Safety Pins** (*Optional*): They may be used for basting the quilt layers together.

❖ **⅜"-wide Masking Tape:** This is used in quilt basting.

❖ **¼"-wide Masking Tape:** This is used to mark quilting lines for hand quilting.

❖ **Plastic-coated Freezer Paper:** This is used for hand appliqué. You can find this item at grocery stores.

> ❖ *Plastic-coated freezer paper comes in handy for making patterns as well as for hand appliqué. It is found in the frozen foods department of your supermarket.*

❖ **Fabric Stabilizer:** You'll need this for machine appliqué.

❖ **Fusible Paper-backed Adhesive:** Great for no-sew appliqué.

❖ **Quilting Hoop:** A 14" to 18" hoop is used for hand quilting.

❖ **Marking Tools:** A fine, hard lead pencil (0.5) should wash out, as should a silver pencil. However, it is always wise to check washability first!

Common Mattress Sizes

Crib: 27" x 52"
Twin: 39" x 75"
Full: 54" x 75"
Queen: 60" x 80"
King: 76" x 80"

CHANGING THE SIZE OF A QUILT

Any of the quilts in this book can easily be made larger or smaller by adding or subtracting blocks. If there are fabric strips between the blocks, these are called sashing. Measure your bed, and decide how far down you want the quilt to hang on the sides (called the "drop"); then add or subtract blocks accordingly. This is done by dividing the block repeat (4", 6", 8", and 12") into the width and length you want your quilt to be. This will give you the number of blocks needed for width and length. If the quilt has sashing or borders, plan them into your measurements.

BASIC CONSTRUCTION TECHNIQUES

Before You Begin

When making a quilt, there are techniques that will aid you in accuracy and make your quilt easier to construct. They are outlined here. As you make the quilts in this book, refer to this chapter when you are unsure how to do something. Specific techniques relevant to the block in a chapter will be covered in that chapter. Happy Quilting!

CUTTING

Most cutting instructions in this book are given for the use of the rotary cutter. When using the rotary cutter, strips are cut across the width of the fabric; then they are cut into squares, triangles, or rectangles. When you are using a mat, rotary cutter, and ruler, always place your cutting board on a table and stand over it while you cut. It will be more comfortable, and you will be able to exert consistent pressure on the rotary cutter. Some projects require the use of templates, which are traced on the fabric and cut out with scissors or a rotary cutter and ruler.

The selvage is trimmed from each side of a fabric before cutting usable patches for a quilt. Most fabric is 44" in width including the selvages but some fabric may be slightly narrower. Once the selvages are removed, you will have a width of between 42½" and 43½". In this book, all required strips are figured using 42" so cutting off the selvages and variation in fabric widths have already been planned into the yardage required.

> ❖ *When you are cutting, make sure the whole piece of fabric is on the table. Fabric hanging over the edge pulls and distorts the fabric that you are cutting on the table.*

Making a Straight-Edge Cut

All instructions are given for right-handed cutting. If you are left-handed, reverse the instructions.

1. Fold the fabric from selvage to selvage. Align the straight of the grain the best you can. Bring the center fold of the fabric to the selvages and align it. You will have four layers.

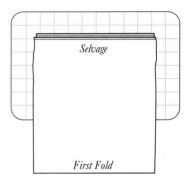

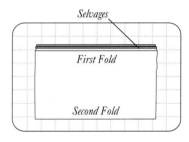

2. Align the 6" side of the ruler with the fold and the selvages. Move the ruler as far as you can to the right and still have four layers of fabric under it. Depress the safety latch on the rotary cutter. Place the fingers of your left hand on the ruler, away from the edge of the ruler. Make a cut starting at the bottom edge and move toward and through the selvages.

Press the cutter firmly but not too heavily as you cut. Put the safety back on the blade after every cut. (Get in the habit of always putting the safety on.) You now have a straight edge to begin your strip cutting. You will follow this procedure on each piece of new fabric that you cut.

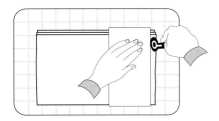

3. Rotate the cutting mat so the fabric layers are on the left-hand side of your board (or walk around the table if you can). The new strip you are cutting needs to be on the left-hand side of the mat.

Cutting Strips

Here are instructions for cutting a strip 4½" x 42". Align the 4½" mark on the ruler at the left edge of the fabric, with the top edge of the ruler parallel to the selvages. To make a cut, press the ruler firmly against the fabric with your entire hand as the cutter slides against the edge of the ruler. Make a cut by placing the rotary cutter at the bottom of the fabric and moving up to the top edge.

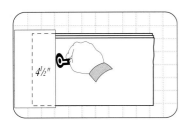

Cutting Squares

Open up the strip of fabric that you just cut. You may stack four rows of strips if you wish. Trim off the selvages.

To cut a square 4½" x 4½", align the top edge of the ruler parallel to the edge of the fabric. Align the 4½" mark on the ruler with the left edge of the fabric. Make a cut.

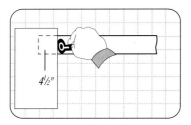

Cutting Half-Square Triangles

Leave the squares stacked. Place the ruler diagonally across the block, matching the edge of the ruler with both corners. Make a cut.

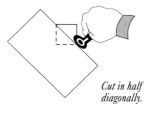

Cut in half diagonally.

Cutting Quarter-Square Triangles

Quarter-square triangles are used along the edges of quilts with a diagonal set. Leave the half-square triangles in place. Lay the ruler across the block to opposite corners and make a cut.

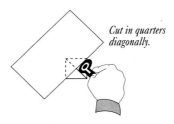

Cut in quarters diagonally.

❖ *When you are cutting several pieces of fabric for a quilt, label the stacks of pieces with "sticky notes." Arrange the pieces in the order they will be stitched. (Example: two half-square triangles that will need to be stitched together are stacked on top of each other and labeled.)*

The Grid Method for Making Half-Square Triangles

When you need to make several half-square triangles, here is a more streamlined way to make them. It was developed by Mary Ellen Hopkins.

1. On the wrong side of the lighter fabric, use an ultra-fine permanent pen to draw a grid with squares that are ⅞" larger than the finished size of the half-square triangle needed. (If you want a 2" finished half-square triangle, the grid should be 2⅞".) Never use fabric larger than an 18" square. It is too hard to handle in the sewing machine and still be accurate.

2. Using your permanent pen, mark diagonal lines as shown. On each side of these lines, draw a dashed line that is ¼" away. The dashed line is the stitching line.

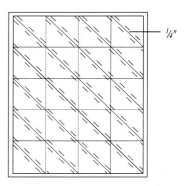

¼"

❖ *Most quilt shops carry printed paper tablets with the grids already drawn, so that you can place a grid on top of your two fabrics and stitch through them without the need to draw the grid first.*

3. Place the right side of this fabric on the right side of the other half-square triangle fabric. Press together lightly. Pin in several places.

4. Stitch on all of the dashed lines. Using your ruler and rotary cutter, cut on the solid square grid lines and on the diagonal lines. You may need to pick out a couple of threads at the points.

5. Open the half-square triangles and press toward the darker side. Trim off points that extend beyond the edge of the block.

Yield: There will be two half-square triangle units from each square drawn on the grid.

> ❖ *Pick up any decorating magazine, and you will see quilts in lots of places besides beds. A large quilt might be displayed on an empty wall; a small quilt might be included in a grouping with other things like baskets, small framed pieces, and so forth. Quilts can adorn only the center of a bed or lie over the back of a chair or be used for a centerpiece on a table. The uses are endless.*

MAKING A TEMPLATE

Templates are patterns for quilt pieces. They are made of plastic or posterboard. You mark around them, then cut out the shape. I like the plastic that looks milky, but which you can see through. It is less slick and easier to control when cutting. Patchwork patterns include seam allowances; appliqué patterns don't.

> ❖ *Always label all templates for quilt block design. Place all the templates that might be used for one pattern in this book in a reclosable bag and label the bag with the name of the quilt, Patchwork Quilts Made Easy, page __. Then if you are making a block at a later time it is always easy to locate the templates.*

Plastic Method

Place the plastic over the pattern in the book. Trace around the template using a ruler on the straight edges. Transfer any markings that are on the template so it is labeled.

Posterboard Method

Place tracing paper over the pattern in the book. Follow the transferring method above. Cut out the paper template, and glue it with rubber cement or glue stick onto posterboard. Then cut out the posterboard.

Using Templates To Cut

Trace around the template onto fabric with a sharp pencil. Cut out with scissors or place the straight edge of a cutting ruler on the pencil line and cut with the rotary cutter. Any curves will need to be cut with scissors.

Fabric can still be stacked as you did before for cutting. Some of the templates face right and some face left. Fold the fabric so right or wrong sides are together and you will automatically get the right side and the left side.

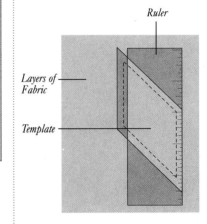

Ruler

Layers of Fabric

Template

SEWING TECHNIQUES

A ¼" seam allowance is always used in piecing unless otherwise indicated. It is the most manageable size where several seams meet, and in patchwork there are many seams! If you stitch a seam even a couple of threads off, the problems add up: the block will be too large or too small. It is extremely worthwhile to check the ¼" seam allowance and be accurate from the very beginning.

To check the ¼" seam allowance, draw a line on a piece of paper ¼" away from the cut edge or use ¼" graph paper. Place the paper under the presser foot of the sewing machine, with the seam allowance to the right, and bring the needle down through the line that you drew. Release the presser foot. Where the edge of the paper ends on the right is the ¼" distance. If it isn't on the edge of your presser foot, then mark the line with a piece of masking tape on your sewing machine. This taped edge will act as your seam gauge to ensure an accurate ¼" seam. You may want to cut a thin piece of moleskin foot and shoe padding and place the sticky side on your sewing machine to mark the ¼" seam allowance. (There is a new foot available that can be adapted to most sewing machines that is called a "Little Foot," which is exactly ¼" wide.)

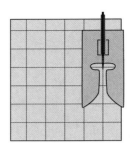

The stitch length should be set at about 14 to 16 stitches to the inch. The stitch has to be wide enough so you can insert your seam ripper. (Of course you won't be doing any ripping.) No back tacking is necessary.

PRESSING

Pressing is very important in any sewing project. In patchwork, the rule is to press both seam allowances toward the darker fabric whenever possible. Where several seams meet, position them so they go in opposite directions. The two seams will nest together when stitched and the points will match. This may mean that one seam isn't pressed toward the darker fabric. The nesting rule applies first.

Use a dry iron when pressing. Press in an up-and-down motion so that the pieces don't become distorted. Press often. Once the blocks are finished, you may use a spray fabric finish while pressing them. This puts a light finish coat on the fabric, and the fabric will hold a press better. The finish, which is not the same as spray starch, is available at supermarkets and hardware stores.

PIECING TECHNIQUES

Chaining

If you are making several blocks, the stitching will go faster if you stitch all of the smaller units together at one time. This is called chaining.

1. Feed pairs of fabric through the sewing machine, one after another, without lifting the presser foot.

2. Remove from the machine and clip the threads between the pairs.

❖ *Alex Anderson of Livermore, California, introduced me to this idea, and I pass it on to all of my students. When starting and ending stitching, take approximately a 1"x 2" scrap of fabric and fold it in half. Stitch through it leaving the presser foot down as you insert the next pair of seams to be stitched. End with another piece of scrap fabric. This eliminates lifting and lowering the presser foot and having to hold onto the threads so they don't bunch up.*

APPLIQUÉ TECHNIQUES

Machine Appliqué

When I am attaching appliqué shapes, I like to use a "stabilizer" behind the background fabric. It eliminates puckering on cotton fabrics and holds everything in place. A stabilizer is a product that looks like non-woven interfacing. After you sew through it, it tears away. I used typing paper before this product was developed, but the stabilizer works much better.

Before you begin, always test your machine's satin stitch on a scrap of fabric, and refer to your sewing machine instruction book if adjustments are necessary.

1. Set the zigzag stitch to almost its full ¹⁄₁₆" width (experiment with your machine), and the stitch length to fine, so the threads will be close together and form a satiny look. Position the needle so that it hits just outside the appliqué shape. Cotton thread or machine embroidery thread will fill in better than polyester thread.

2. Begin on a straight edge. As you reach a curve or rounded area, don't force the fabric to turn. It will turn gently on its own with a little guidance from you.

3. To stitch a heart's center notch, stitch into the notch the width of the stitch, leaving the needle in. Then lift the presser foot and turn the fabric to continue.

The more you practice machine appliqué, the more your technique will improve. Learning to feed the fabric and letting it flow gently are the keys for smooth stitching. After a shape is appliquéd, you may wish to top-stitch details shown on the pattern.

Hand Appliqué

The freezer-paper method of hand appliqué is easy to do. I teach beginners this method because they can master it quickly.

1. Trace the appliqué shapes onto the non-coated side of the freezer paper. Cut the shapes out along the traced line. Iron the paper shapes on the right side of the fabric, with the plastic-coated side down.

2. Trim around the shapes, adding a ³⁄₁₆" seam allowance. Clip any inside points as needed.

Clip fabric.

Freezer Paper

3. Working from the wrong side of the background fabric, pin the appliqué shape in place. (This way, you won't catch the appliqué thread on the pins.)

4. Turn under the seam allowance, an inch at a time, with your fingertips.

5. Cut a thread approximately 18" long. Thread one end into a needle and knot the other end. To begin stitching, bring the needle up from the underside, catching the folded edge of the appliqué shape.

Bring the needle back down, carrying the thread across the fabric back approximately ⅛" before bringing it to the top again. The threads on the back of the fabric should not be more than ¼" apart. This method of sewing is called a blind stitch.

6. To make a point, fold the tip as shown, then fold the sides.

View From Wrong Side of Fabric

7. Clip inside corners to within ¹⁄₁₆" of the freezer paper. Run the edge of the needle along the fabric edges and it will help to pull the threads underneath. Tack at the very center.

8. Remove the freezer paper.

> ❖ *Your needle is your best friend in appliqué. Use it to turn under the seam allowance. Run it underneath a curve to distribute the seam allowance evenly.*

Fusible Appliqué

Use fusible paper-backed adhesive to fuse shapes on quilt blocks. If you plan to sew through the appliqués, purchase sewable webbing only. The yardage requirements were figured using 17"-wide adhesive.

1. Trace the appliqué shapes on the paper side of the adhesive. They can be close together.

2. Follow the manufacturer's instructions and fuse the adhesive to the back side of the fabric.

3. Cut around the edges of the appliqués, cutting on the tracing line.

4. Peel the paper off the fabric. Position an appliqué on the background square and press it in place, following the manufacturer's instructions. The appliqués can be left as is or stitched in place. If a quilt will get a lot of use, I stitch the appliqués down. Either a machine hemstitch, narrow zigzag, or hand buttonhole stitch will hold the appliqué in place. Use monofilament thread or cotton thread that matches the appliqué in the top of the machine and cotton thread in the bobbin. If you choose to stitch around the appliqués, do so before you sew the blocks together.

BUTTON CLUSTERS

Look closely at the buttons in the *Lacy Fans* quilt photo on page 147 to get ideas for composing with buttons. I used to use only old pearl buttons, but now I have expanded my techniques and use all kinds of buttons. Sometimes, the back sides of the old pearl buttons are more interesting than the fronts. When you embellish with buttons, it will be necessary to purchase them in bulk or from junk or antique stores. If they are dirty, put them in hot soapy water in a jar and swish them around to loosen the dirt. You may need to do this a couple of times. Let them dry on paper towels.

You will want a variety of button sizes from ¼" to 1". This will make the clusters more interesting. I like a variety of styles, too, to add texture. Always use double thread knotted at the end. Stitch through each button twice and knot on the back before going on to the next button. This way, if any single button comes loose, you won't lose them all. Start by stitching one button down. Bring up the needle right beside the edge of the button you just finished stitching. Stitch the second button in place. It will automatically overlap the first button.

STITCHING THE BLOCKS TOGETHER

Straight Set

Each quilt illustration will show you how the blocks are stitched together. Many combinations are stitched together in straight rows, sometimes alternating design (pieced or appliquéd) blocks with plain blocks; then the rows are joined. This is called a straight set.

Always lay out the quilt blocks before you begin sewing so that you can be sure they are in a pleasing order. Stitch the blocks together in horizontal rows. Press seam allowances toward the right on odd-numbered rows and toward the left on even-numbered rows when applicable. Then join row 2 to row 1, row 3 to row 2, and so on. When you join the rows, the seam allowances that you pressed in opposite directions will automatically nest together.

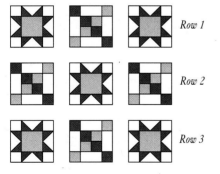

Row 1

Row 2

Row 3

Diagonal Set

In a diagonal set, the rows run across the quilt at a 45° angle (on point). Setting triangles fill in around the edges, and smaller corner triangles fill in the four corners of the quilt top. Always lay out the blocks before you begin sewing to be sure they are in a pleasing order. Sew blocks into diagonal rows including the appropriate setting triangles on the ends. Press seam allowances in one direction for row 1 and in the opposite direction for row 2 so that the seams will nest together when joining rows. The corner triangles are added last.

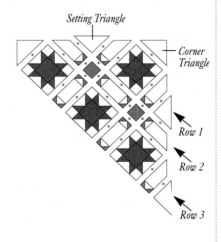

Setting Triangle

Corner Triangle

Row 1

Row 2

Row 3

ADDING BORDERS

Borders can act as a frame for pieced and appliquéd quilts. To attach a border strip, start at one side of the quilt. Lay the right side of the border strip on the right side of the quilt and pin the two layers together. With the back facing you, stitch ¼" from the edge, making sure that seam allowances are sewn down in the direction that you originally pressed them. Press both seam allowances toward the border. Repeat for the other side of the quilt. If there are corner pieces, add them to each end of the top and bottom borders. Add the top and bottom border strips using the same process as the sides.

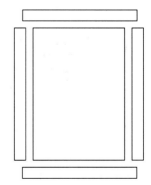

❖ When adding a border to a quilt, find the middle on one side edge and place a pin there. On long borders, repeat this three times. Do the same on the quilt top. Match up the pins. Then, if there is any easing necessary, it will be evenly divided along the border's edge.

Mitering Border Corners

1. Use the patterns below to cut a 45° angle at each end of the strips.

Borders will look like this.

2. With a pencil, mark the dots from the patterns onto the wrong side of the border strips. With right sides together, place the border strips atop the quilt. Position the border strip dots ¼" in from the corner and pin.

3. Sew one side of the border to the quilt at a time, sewing from dot to dot and STOP; back-tack one stitch at the beginning and at the end. When you add the next border to the quilt, the dots will match up in the corner. Always sew to the dot and STOP.

4. To join the mitered corner, place the two corners together and sew from the dot to the outer edge. Press open.

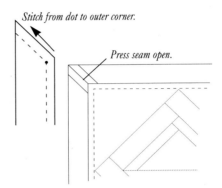

Stitch from dot to outer corner.

Press seam open.

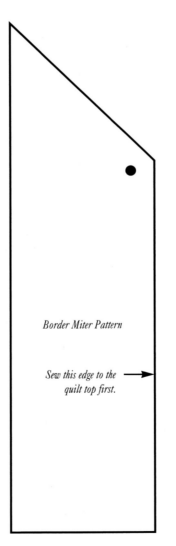

Border Miter Pattern

Sew this edge to the quilt top first.

Border Miter Pattern

Sew this edge to the quilt top first.

❖ *Spray starch your fabric (unless it is flannel) before cutting if it feels unstable. This puts a finish on the fabric that will make it easier to cut. It can be used on a finished block also. Spray starch works well on backing fabric when you are going to machine quilt. The extra finish makes the fabric easier to manipulate in the machine.*

FINISHING THE QUILT

Marking the Quilt Design

If you need to mark any quilt designs before quilting, check the washability of your pencil on a scrap of fabric first. Heat will set most pencil marks, so do not press the fabric after marking. If the fabrics have not been pre-washed, sometimes the pencil marks will not wash out. There are fabric erasers, available in the notions section of fabric and quilt shops, which will remove most pencil marks.

Your rotary cutting ruler is convenient for marking straight quilting lines. If any marking for quilting is necessary, do the marking before you layer the quilt. Quarter-inch masking tape is available at fabric stores and quilt shops. Use it to mark straight stitching lines after layering the quilt sandwich. Stitch along the edge of the tape. Then remove the tape, and reuse it. (Don't leave tape on the top any longer than necessary to quilt along its edge to avoid leaving a sticky residue.)

There are also numerous stencils with quilting motifs available at your local stores. You trace around some; others are paper that can be stitched through and torn away. In quilts that have a light-colored background, the pattern may be placed under the fabric and the design traced. Or use a light table for dark-colored fabrics.

Layering and Basting the Quilt

Prepare the backing by sewing any seams to make a piece large enough for the quilt (see individual quilt instructions). I have planned the batting and backing to be at least two inches larger than the finished size all around. Trim excess as required.

Bed sheets can be used for quilt backing in some cases. Since they have a high thread count, they are difficult to hand quilt, but they can be quilted easily by machine. Flannel is a good backing for baby and juvenile quilts since the nap makes it stick to the bed.

Layering and basting needs to be done on a hard surface, either a large table or the floor.

1. Place the backing wrong side up on the surface. Use the ⅝"-wide masking tape and tape each corner to the surface, making sure the fabric is taut. Then tape the centers of each side and work toward the corners. Tape about every 12".

Taping Quilt Back

2. Place the batting over the backing. Do not stretch or distort, although it may need straightening and patting down.

3. Lay the quilt top right side up over the batting, centering it on the batting and backing. Smooth it out.

4. Basting may be done with safety pins or thread. To safety-pin baste, start at the center and pin about every 8" to 10".

To baste with a thread, use a large embroidery needle and a single thread knotted at the end. See the next illustration, and start from the center, taking large stitches to the sides. Knot the thread at the end. Start from the center each time.

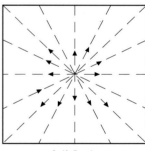

Quilt Basting

Or the quilt may be basted in a grid with lines 4" apart.

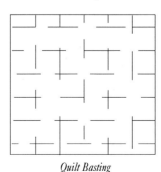

Quilt Basting

QUILTING

Directions are given for machine and hand quilting. While you may use either method, most of the quilts in this book are machine-quilted. Always do a practice test on layered fabric if you are machine quilting to make sure your machine is in good working order.

Quilting by Machine

If your machine has a walking foot or even-feed foot, you will find machine quilting much easier. There are three layers to be fed under the foot, and the top layer can easily drag. The walking foot feeds all three layers evenly.

Most of the quilts in this book are stitched "in-the-ditch" first. No marking is necessary because the stitching follows the seam lines and is as close to the seam as possible on the side of the seam without seam allowances.

Stitch in-the-ditch as close to the seam as possible.

Use this method to stitch around blocks and borders. I recommend doing this first, then marking other quilting designs. That way, your marked designs won't rub off during quilting. Then decorative quilting can be done in the other spaces. Any specific quilting instructions appear with the individual quilt directions. Remove the basting or pins as you finish quilting in each area.

1. When machine quilting, put your machine on a large table or place a card table in front of your machine. As the quilt feeds through the machine, it can rest on the table instead of pulling over the edge. If you are quilting a large quilt, you may find it necessary to roll the side of the quilt that goes under the arm of the machine.

2. Thread either monofilament or cotton thread through the top of your machine and cotton thread in the bobbin to match the back of the quilt.

3. At the beginning and ending of each line of stitching, secure the threads by back-tacking two stitches. Clip threads as you finish each seam.

4. To stitch in-the-ditch, line up the quilt so it can feed straight through the machine. Spread the seam with your fingers as you stitch, and stitch as close to the seam as possible. When you move your hands away, the fabric relaxes and hides the stitching. When all the quilting is finished, remove the basting stitches.

Hand Quilting

Hand quilting is done with a short, sharp needle called a "between." Betweens start at size 8, the largest needle, and go to a 12. The consistency of the size of the stitches is more important than having tiny stitches. The thickness of the batting helps to determine whether the stitches are small or not. As you practice and do more quilting, your stitches will become smaller and more consistent.

Hand quilting was done traditionally ¼" from the seam lines. The larger spaces would have a design quilted in them. To find stencils for quilting designs, visit your local quilt shop. Use the ¼" masking tape along the edge of the seam as a guide for hand quilting ¼" away. The tape is reusable four to five times.

Most people find it easiest to quilt using a hoop. The three layers are held taut, and it is easier to get consistent stitches. Traditionally hoops were round, but you now see the PVC pipe square frames that work well as you near the corners. There is also a half hoop that lets you quilt right up to the edge of the quilt. Large floor frames are still used for large quilts, but many of today's homes do not have room to leave a frame set up for any length of time.

1. Use a single thread about 18" long and knotted at one end. To secure the knot under the top layer of the fabric, take a single stitch, through the top layer only, toward where you will begin quilting.

Pull the thread slightly until the knot opens the weave of the fabric and slips through. The knot pops through more easily if you put the needle between two of the fabric threads.

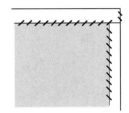

Pull the knot through the top layer only.

2. The quilting stitch is an up-and-down motion. Insert the needle from the top to the back side, making a stitch an eighth to a tenth of an inch long. As you get the feel of it, you will be able to get several stitches on the needle. I find that it takes me about 15 minutes to get into the rhythm of quilting each time I pick it up. The finer the needle and the thinner the batting, the smaller the stitch. A thimble will be very helpful, also.

Stitch.

3. When you reach the end of a line of quilting, make a single knot in the thread.

4. Take a small stitch through the top layer only and pull the knot through the fabric. Trim off the excess thread and remove the basting. It takes practice to master the quilting stitch.

BINDING

Binding is cut on the crosswise grain for all quilts in this book.

1. Refer to the specific quilt you are making to find out how long to make the strips for each edge.

2. Stitch the binding strips together into one long length, then cut the specific lengths needed.

3. Place the side binding strip along the edge of the quilt, with right sides together, and sew ¼" from the edge. Use your walking foot or even-feed foot to avoid puckers or creeping fabric.

4. Trim off the excess batting and backing to match the ¼" seam allowance.

5. Press the raw edge of the binding under ¼".

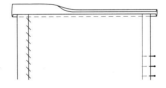

6. Fold the binding to the back of the quilt and line up the folded edge of the binding with the seam line you just stitched to hand-sew the binding to the quilt. Pin every few inches.

7. Slipstitch the side binding to the back of the quilt.

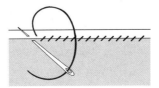

8. Repeat Steps 3–7 for the remaining side, top, and bottom bindings. At the corners, fold under the raw edges of the top and bottom bindings even with the side bindings and hand sew.

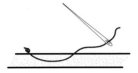

Tuck under seam allowances and stitch.

❖ *Sign your quilt to document who made it and the year it was made. If it is for a special person or occasion, document that, too. You may want to add special information or a personal message. You can make a label out of light-colored fabric and write on it with a permanent pen, or you can embroider or cross-stitch a label. Sometimes, I choose a quilt block that didn't fit on the front of the quilt, write on it, and put it on the back.*

Chapter Three

NINE PATCH
QUILTS

CHAPTER THREE

Nine Patch Quilts

Nine Patch quilt blocks are some of the simplest blocks to make as you can see from the photographs in this chapter. The basic block consists of nine equal-sized squares. They can appear simplistic, dramatic, or more complex depending on the composition. All of these quilts incorporate the Nine Patch block whether set straight or on the diagonal.

Victorian Melody uses a beautiful large-scale floral fabric for its theme. This fabric is the companion or alternate block set next to the Nine Patches in the quilt. When you use a large floral and cut the blocks out, no two will be exactly alike thus creating a flowing, garden-like setting. Notice how the lavender squares in the Nine Patch create paths up and down and across the quilt like a trellis.

If you have always wanted to make a scrap quilt then *Nine By Nine* is a good place to start. I love the nostalgic look of old fabrics that have a mellow tan background. Today's manufacturers are creating more and more of this look in fabrics. Take note of the brighter reds and the duller reds, which really make the quilt work. The subtle stripe border adds an extra dimension to all of the quiet print fabrics.

At first glance it is difficult to believe that *Amish Barn Raising* is a Nine Patch design, but it is! My quilting friend Joanne Myers introduced me to this arrangement. Nine different fabrics have been used in the block; the overall shape occurs because of the contrast in the fabric choices. There are three lights, five darks, and one bright. The blocks are then turned in each row to create the design. If you decide to use prints, just remember that the contrast is very important to make the design show up.

Garden Gate was made as an entry by Andrea Balosky for a *Patchwork Quilts Made Easy* quilt contest at my store. It won first place! Upon viewing it, I felt I was surrounded by a garden full of summer flowers. Notice how the light squares in the Nine Patch create a trellis effect. The companion blocks start out as a large floral in the center; a round of green is added, then a round of very light floral and two rounds of darker floral. Andrea is a scrap-quilt maker *par excellence*. At the store we save all of our little pieces for her. Later we see them appear in her quilt creations.

In planning this quilt you can use a variety of different fabrics that are all the same value in a round, as Andrea has, or just use one fabric. If you are unsure about which fabric is which value, put little swatches in the copy machine to get a black-and-white version that shows the contrast immediately.

NINE PATCH BLOCK INSTRUCTIONS

Enjoy the Nine Patch experience! Let it be a stepping-off point to creating your own Nine Patch variations. Read through all of the general instructions before you begin these projects.

Making the Nine Patch Block

Let's start with a two-color block. It is made up of a Unit 1 and a Unit 2, and, there will always be twice as many Unit 1's as there are Unit 2's.

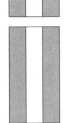

1. Unit 1: Stitch three strips together—dark, light, dark. Make two sets of these.

Unit 1

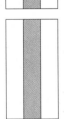

2. Unit 2: Stitch three strips together—light, dark, light. Make one set.

3. Press all seams toward the darker strips. Trim to square up short edges.

Unit 2

4. Cut across the strips as shown.

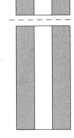

- - - - - - - - *Cut*

The width of the cut strip will be the same width as the individual strips that make up the unit. For example, if you began with a 2½" strip, the width of the cut will be 2½".

5. To construct the block, place right sides together of a Unit 1 and a Unit 2. The seams will automatically nest together. Stitch. Stitch a second Unit 1 on the other side of Unit 2 (see below). Press both seams in one direction. This process is one form of strip-piecing.

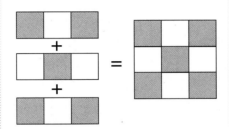

Scrap Nine Patch Blocks for the Nine by Nine Quilt

1. To cut individual squares to use in the Nine Patch, first cut strips of several fabrics.

2. Stack the strips four to six deep. Cut out the squares.

3. Scatter the squares randomly on a table, and start picking them up two at a time and placing them in a Nine Patch design. I pick up one square and look for a friend for it—another fabric that has something in common with the first. Once the nine squares are in place, evaluate the arrangement and make changes if necessary.

4. First, pick up row 2 squares and place them right sides together on top of row 1 squares. Stitch through the three sets of squares leaving a chain of thread between. (Do not cut the chains.)

5. Open these stitched squares and lay them back down on the table. Place row 3 squares on top of row 2 right sides together. Stitch through these as you did before.

6. Press the seam allowances in rows 1 and 3 in one direction and row 2 in the opposite direction. Stitch the first row to the second, and the second one to the third. Press.

VICTORIAN MELODY

The finished size is 65½" x 91". The block size is 6".

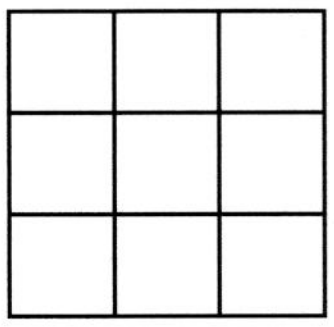

Refer to quilt drawing and photo for color placement.

SUPPLIES

CUTTING GUIDE

Main Print for Companion Blocks, Setting Triangles, Corner Triangles, Second Border, and Patch C
3⅛ yards

Main-Print Companion Blocks: Cut seven strips 6½" x 42".
Open the strips, stack, and trim off selvages. Cut 40 squares 6½" x 6½".
Setting Triangles: Cut seven squares 9¾" x 9¾".
Cut into quarters diagonally. 26 are required.
Corner Triangles: Cut two squares 5⅛" x 5⅛". Cut in half diagonally.
Second Border's Patches A and D: Cut seven strips 5½" x 42".
Join into one long strip. From this strip cut two Patch D's 51½";
cut two A's 77".
Second Border's Patch C: Cut four squares 5½" x 5½".

Dark Patches in Nine Patch
1⅓ yards

Dark Patches: Cut 18 strips 2½" x 42".

Light Patches in Nine Patch
1⅛ yards

Light Patches: Cut 15 strips 2½" x 42".

First Border, Patch B, and Binding
1⅛ yards

First Border: Cut seven strips 2½" x 42". Join into one long strip.
From this strip cut two strips 77" for the sides; cut two strips 55½"
for the top and bottom.
Second Border's Patch B: Cut eight rectangles 2½" x 5½".
Binding: Cut eight strips 1¾" x 42". Join into one long strip.
From this strip cut two strips 91" for the sides; cut two strips 66"
for the top and bottom.

Backing
5⅓ yards

Backing: Cut two pieces 95" x 42". Trim off selvages and sew sections
together, right sides facing, along the lengthwise grain.

Batting 70" x 95"

Sewing instructions begin on next page.

SEWING INSTRUCTIONS FOR VICTORIAN MELODY

Review the Quilting Basics in Chapter 2 before you begin.

1. Follow the block construction directions on page 41 and sew seven sets of strips for Unit 1 and four sets of strips for Unit 2.

2. Construct 54 Nine Patch blocks.

3. Arrange the blocks, setting triangles, and corner triangles on a bed or table. Follow the diagonal set instructions on page 33 for sewing the blocks together.

4. Follow the instructions on page 33 for adding the first border.

5. To add the second border, follow the illustration below. For the sides, add a Patch B to each end of A. Make two. Sew one to each side of quilt. For the top and bottom, add a Patch B to each end of D; add Patch C to the remaining side of each B. Make two of these and join one to the top and the other to the bottom of the quilt.

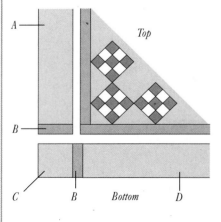

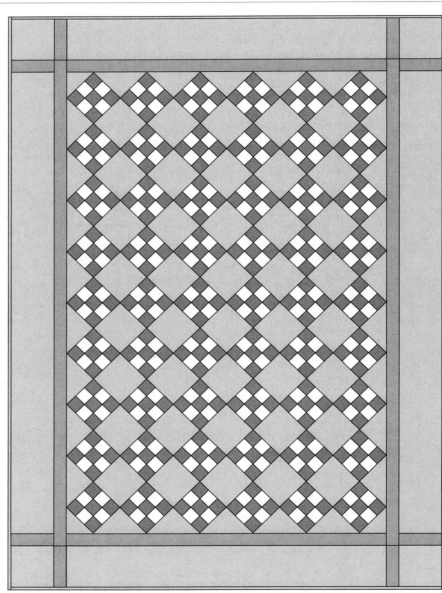

Victorian Melody Quilt Drawing

6. Follow the instructions on page 35 for basting the quilt.

7. This quilt was machine-quilted diagonally along the block seam, then in-the-ditch on the border seams.

8. Follow the instructions on page 37 for binding the quilt.

NINE BY NINE

The finished size is 33" x 33". The block size is 6".

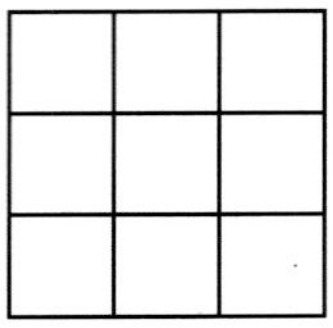

Refer to quilt drawing and photo for color placement.

SUPPLIES

CUTTING

Several Prints for Color 1 in Nine Patch Blocks ¼ yard total	**Nine Patches:** Cut both colors of fabric into strips 2½" x 42". Layer into stacks of four. Cut into 81 squares 2½" x 2½".
Several Prints for Color 2 in Nine Patch Blocks ¼ yard total	
Companion Blocks, Setting Triangles, and Corner Triangles ⅜ yard each of three fabrics (1⅛ yards total)	**Companion Blocks:** Cut four squares 6½" x 6½". **Setting Triangles:** Cut two squares 9¾" x 9¾". Cut into quarters diagonally. **Corner Triangles:** Cut two squares 5⅛" x 5⅛". Cut in half diagonally.
First Border ⅛ yard	**First Border:** Cut three strips 1" x 42". Join into one long strip. From this strip cut two strips 26" for the sides; cut two strips 27" for the top and bottom.
Second Border ¼ yard	**Second Border:** Cut three strips 1½" x 42". Join into one long strip. From this strip cut two strips 27" for the sides; cut two strips 29" for the top and bottom.
Third Border and Binding ½ yard	**Third Border:** Cut three strips 2½" x 42". Join into one long strip. From this strip cut two strips 29" for the sides; cut two strips 33" for the top and bottom. **Binding:** Cut four strips 1¾" x 42". From these strips cut two strips 33" for the sides; cut two strips 33½" for the top and bottom.
Backing 1⅛ yards	**Backing:** Cut one piece 37" x 37".
Batting 37" x 37"	

SEWING INSTRUCTIONS FOR NINE BY NINE

Review the Quilting Basics in Chapter 2 before you begin.

1. Arrange the Nine Patch squares randomly and make nine blocks following the instructions on page 41.

2. Follow the diagonal set instructions on page 33 for sewing the blocks together.

3. Follow the instructions on page 33 for adding the borders.

4. Follow the instructions on page 35 for basting the quilt.

5. This quilt is machine-quilted diagonally each way 2" apart creating a 2" grid.

6. Following the instructions on page 37 for binding the quilt.

Nine by Nine Quilt Drawing

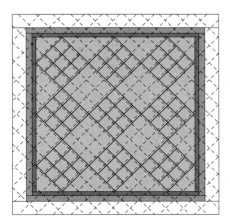

Quilting Design

❖ All of the squares for the Nine Patches were cut separately to create a scrap-quilt look. When you look at the quilt, you basically see two colors, red and blue. As long as your fabrics have something in common, you can use a lot of prints and still have continuity. When buying fabric for quilts like this, purchase ⅛-yard cuts so you can collect a variety. Notice the use of the stripes and plaids. They add interest to all of the florals.

AMISH BARN RAISING

The finished size is 60½" x 60½". The block size is 6".

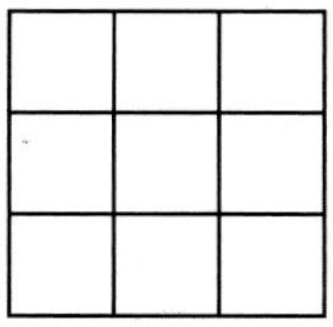

Refer to quilt drawing and photo for color placement.

SUPPLIES

Nine Patch Blocks:
Three different lights
⅝ yard each

Five different darks
⅝ yard each

One bright
⅝ yard

Binding
⅓ yard

Backing
3¾ yards

Batting 65" x 65"

CUTTING

Nine Patch Blocks: Cut seven strips of each light, dark, and bright fabric, 2½" x 42".

Binding: Cut six strips, 1¾" x 42". Join into one long strip. From this strip cut two strips 60½" for the sides; cut two strips 61" for the top and bottom.

Backing: Cut two pieces 65" x 42". Trim off the selvages and sew sections together, right sides facing, along the lengthwise grain.

Sewing instructions begin on next page.

SEWING INSTRUCTIONS FOR AMISH BARN RAISING

Review the Quilting Basics in Chapter 2 before you begin.

1. Using the block drawing (below) as your guide, decide on the placement of colors and mark them on the block chart. I use colored pencils.

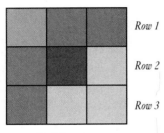

Block Drawing

Row 1	magenta	dark green	purple
Row 2	royal blue	black	pink
Row 3	dark red	lavender	yellow

bright	dark	dark	Row 1
dark	dark	light	Row 2
dark	light	light	Row 3

Block Chart

2. Sew the strips together in seven sets of three separate rows. Press the first row to the right, the second to the left, and the third to the right.

3. Cut across the strips at 2½" intervals.

Amish Barn Raising Quilt Drawing

4. Refer to the basic block construction on page 41 to complete the blocks. There will be 100 blocks.

5. Arrange the blocks in rows, following the quilt photo. Follow the straight set instructions on page 33 for sewing the blocks together.

6. Follow the instructions on page 35 for basting the quilt.

7. The illustration to the right shows the quilting pattern used on this quilt. Continue quilting by following the diagonal bands of color from the center outward.

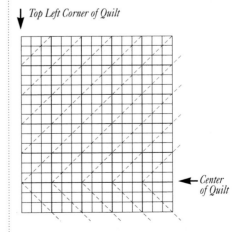

↓ *Top Left Corner of Quilt*

← *Center of Quilt*

8. Follow instructions on page 37 for binding the quilt.

GARDEN GATE

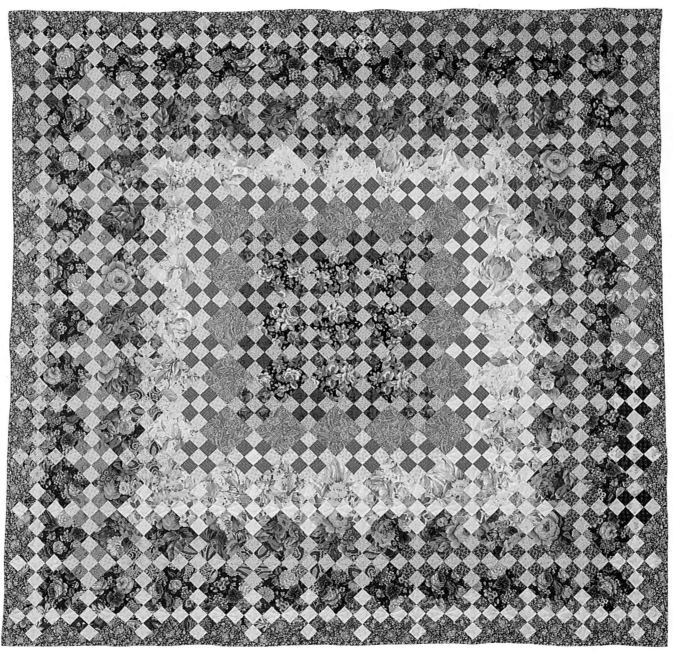

The finished size is 77" x 77". The block size is 4½".

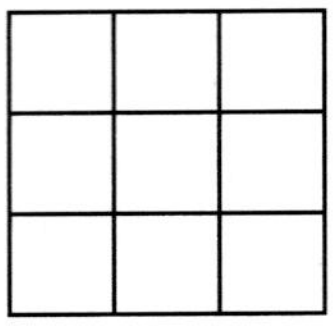

Refer to quilt drawing and photo for color placement. The following chart has been devised to help you in color placement. It matches the quilt drawing.

SUPPLIES

Nine Patch Blocks:
¾ yard light,
2 yards medium light,
and 1½ yards medium dark (Total yardage is given; choose several fabrics if you want a scrap look.)

Companion Blocks:
½ yard medium light,
⅜ yard medium, and
1⅔ yards medium dark

CUTTING

Rounds (blocks needed): Cut the 5" strips into squares 5" x 5" for Companion blocks. Follow the instructions on page 41 to make Nine Patch blocks using the 2" strips. Use the lighter of the two colors for the corners and center of the Nine Patch blocks.
(ML= medium light, MD= medium dark, L= light, M= medium)

Round 1	ML one strip	2" x 42"	4 Squares	
	MD one strip	2" x 32"		
Round 2	MD one square	5" x 5"	9 Squares	
	one strip	5" x 42"		
Round 3	ML three strips	2" x 42"	12 Squares	
	MD two strips	2" x 42"		
	one strip	2" x 16"		
Round 4	M two strips	5" x 42"	16 Squares	
Round 5	L five strips	2" x 42"	20 Squares	
	MD four strips	2" x 42"		
Round 6	ML three strips	5" x 42"	24 Squares	
Round 7	L seven strips	2" x 42"	28 Squares	
	ML five strips	2" x 42"		
	one strip	2" x 24"		
Round 8	MD four strips	5" x 42"	32 Squares	
Round 9	ML nine strips	2" x 42"	36 Squares	
	MD seven strips	2" x 42"		
	one strip	2" x 8"		
Round 10	MD five strips	5" x 42"	40 Squares	
Round 11	ML eleven strips	2" x 42"	44 Squares	
	MD eight strips	2" x 42"		
	one strip	2" x 32"		

Setting and Corner Triangles
⅔ yard medium dark

Setting Triangles: Cut two MD strips 7⅝" x 42".
From these strips cut 11 squares 7⅝" x 7⅝".
Cut one more square 7⅝" x 7⅝". Cut into quarters diagonally.
Corner Triangles: Cut two MD squares 4⅛" x 4⅛".
Cut in half diagonally.

Binding
½ yard medium dark

Binding: Cut eight MD strips 1¾" x 42". Join into one long strip.
From this strip cut two strips 77" for the sides; cut two strips 77½" for the top and bottom.

Backing
4⅝ yards

Backing: Cut two pieces 42" x 81". Trim off the selvages and sew sections together, right sides facing, along the lengthwise grain.

Batting 81" x 81"

SEWING INSTRUCTIONS FOR GARDEN GATE

Review the Quilting Basics in Chapter 2 before you begin.

1. Following the Nine Patch block instructions on page 41, make the blocks for each round, as indicated on the chart.

2. Follow the quilt drawing and lay out the blocks. Follow the diagonal set instructions on page 33 for sewing the blocks together.

3. Follow the instructions on page 35 for basting the quilt.

4. This quilt was hand-quilted on the diagonal, but it could be easily machine-quilted.

5. Following the instructions on page 37 for binding the quilt.

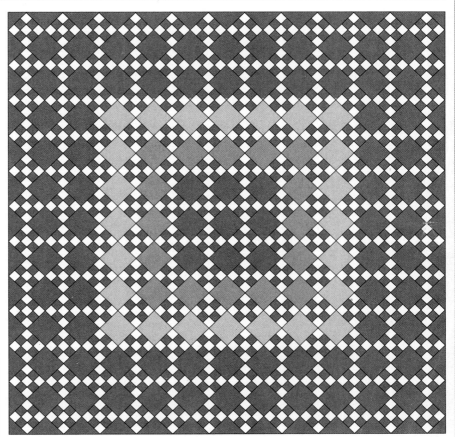

Garden Gate Quilt Drawing

Odd-numbered rounds are not labeled.

Chapter Four
PINWHEEL QUILTS

CHAPTER FOUR

Pinwheel Quilts

Pinwheels spin, tip, and turn to create movement in any quilt design. The whimsical feeling they create reminds us of children running and playing with their pinwheel toys. I am sure our great-grandmothers had that in mind when they thought up the Pinwheel quilt pattern. The block is easy to construct, and the possibilities for design variations are endless as you can see in the quilts that are pictured.

The block can be broken down into four squares. Each square is made up of contrasting triangles. Because all of the points meet at the center, the dark-and-light contrast creates a spinning effect.

The half-square triangle unit also can be used in a border design. In *Flying Geese Pinwheels* a row of half-square triangles are joined on either side of a strip to create the Flying Geese. Notice the diagonal feeling that is created when the blocks are placed next to a companion block. Red-and-white quilts as well as blue-and-white quilts have an everlasting appeal.

Starry Pinwheels is a scrap quilt with a modern look. It lends itself well to using a collection of different fabrics in a predetermined color scheme. Several different blues and reds and yellows are used for the pinwheels. Within the blue range, there are navy stars, bright blue vines, a dark blue swirl print, and a medium blue star. As long as the fabrics have something in common, they will work together. In the background, I used either black or muslin or a black-and-white check. By varying the background slightly, you will add more visual interest.

The soft and bright tones of three colors are used with black in *Amish Pinwheels*. This quilt sparkles and glows with movement from a distance. There are two sizes of Pinwheel blocks used in the quilt pattern. To create the border, large half-square triangle blocks were placed around the edge.

The *Hour Glass Pinwheels* quilt with pink and teal fabrics looks like a baby quilt to me. It has a soft playful look to it. The blocks were made with a variety of pinks and teals so some are brighter than others. The background is constant. Once the blocks are finished, play around with their placement. This is what Barbara Slater did when she made it. The bright pinks create an hour glass appearance and don't look like pinwheels at all.

The accent strip of bright pink helps to define the body of the quilt and separate it from the border. The border units are half-square triangle blocks half the size of the Pinwheel blocks. The colors are scattered randomly around the edge.

PINWHEEL BLOCK INSTRUCTIONS

Take another step into easy quiltmaking with Pinwheel Quilts, which divide simple squares in half diagonally.
Read through all of the general instructions before you begin these projects.

    Each block is made up of four contrasting half-square triangles units. The *Flying Geese Pinwheels* quilt on page 58 takes very little planning, since it contains only two colors.

1. Pick up a pair of patches (pinwheel and background). *Always keep the pinwheel fabric on the top and background fabric on the bottom.* Stitch pairs together along the longer side (bias edge).

 **2.** Feed the pairs of patches through the sewing machine, one after the other, without lifting the presser foot. There will be a small chain of stitches between the units, creating a string of stitched units.

3. Remove the chain of patches from the machine. Clip the threads between the pairs to release them. Press both seam allowances toward the darker of the fabrics.

 Trim **4.** Trim off the points even with the edge of the block for easier quilt assembly. *Trim*

 + =
 + =

5. Lay four blocks out beside the sewing machine as shown here.

6. Pick up the top two blocks and place them right sides together. The seam allowances will automatically nest together. Stitch the seam. (When you are making the quilt, you can feed the blocks through the sewing machine continuously without cutting the thread until they are all sewn.)

7. To complete the block, place right sides together of two of the two-block units, letting the seam allowances nest together in the center, one seam allowance to the right and one to the left. Always be sure the points are toward the center of the block. Press the seam allowances in one direction.

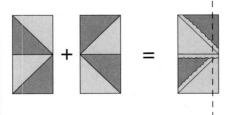

❖ *The simplest way to construct Pinwheel blocks is to cut a strip of fabric of each of the pinwheel colors. Open the strips and place a pinwheel strip on top of a background strip, right sides together, to cut the squares and half-square triangles. Then, when the triangles are picked up, they are ready to sew together. Be sure not to stretch the bias edges. Two pairs of strips can be stacked up and cut at the same time. In the individual quilt descriptions, more specific stacking instructions will be given. (If you have several half-square triangles to make, it would be faster to use the grid method on page 28.)*

FLYING GEESE PINWHEELS

The finished size is 88½" x 112½". The block size is 6".

Refer to quilt drawing and photo for color placement.

SUPPLIES

CUTTING

Main Color (red) for Pinwheels, Border, and Binding
4¾ yards

Background Color (white) for Pinwheels, Companion Blocks, Borders, and Corner Blocks
7¼ yards

Pinwheel Blocks: Cut 23 strips 3⅞" x 42" of each color. Open the strips and stack pairs of red and white strips, right sides together, with the red on top. Make five stacks of four each and one stack of three. Cut into 222 squares 3⅞" x 3⅞". Cut the squares in half diagonally, and leave these stacked for easy pick-up when you begin to sew.
Companion Blocks: Cut 19 white strips 6½" x 42". Open the strips and stack them in groups of four. Cut 110 squares 6½" x 6½".
Border: Cut 13 strips 2⅞" x 42" of each color. Repeat the stacking process explained above for the Pinwheel block. Cut 180 squares of each color 2⅞" x 2⅞". Cut the squares in half diagonally.
Border's Center Band: Cut 10 red strips 1½" x 42".
Corner Blocks: Cut four white squares 5½" x 5½".
Binding: Cut 10 red strips 1¾" x 42". Join into one long strip. From this strip cut two strips 112½" for the sides; cut two strips 89" for the top and bottom.

Backing
7¾ yards

Backing: Cut three pieces of fabric 93" x 42". Trim off the selvages and sew sections together, right sides facing, along the lengthwise grain.

Batting 93" x 117"

Sewing instructions begin on next page.

SEWING INSTRUCTIONS FOR FLYING GEESE PINWHEELS

Review the Quilting Basics in Chapter 2 before you begin.

1. Following the basic block instructions on page 57, make 111 Pinwheel blocks.

2. Arrange the Pinwheel blocks with the Companion blocks in the straight-set design explained on page 33. There are 17 vertical rows. Each odd-numbered row contains seven Pinwheels and six Companion blocks. Each even-numbered row contains six Pinwheels and seven Companion blocks.

3. Follow the straight set instructions on page 33 for sewing the blocks together.

4. For the border, follow steps 1 through 4 in the Pinwheel Block Instructions on page 57, and make 360 half-square triangle blocks.

5. For the side borders, join four rows of 51 units each. For the top and bottom, you will need to sew together four rows of 39 units each.

6. Stitch the center band border strips into one long piece. Cut two strips 78½" long for the top and bottom and two 102½" long for the sides.

7. Stitch the pieced borders on each side of the center band.

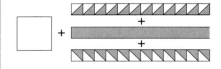

8. Press seams toward the center band.

Flying Geese Pinwheels Quilt Drawing

9. Add the corner blocks to each end of the top and bottom borders.

10. Follow the instructions on page 33 for adding the borders.

11. Follow the instructions on page 35 for basting the quilt.

12. First quilt in-the-ditch in all block seams, Pinwheel seams, and border seams. Use the template given here to trace for the machine-quilted design in the center of each Companion block.

13. Follow the instructions on page 37 for binding the quilt.

Quilting Design for Companion Blocks
Flying Geese Pinwheel Quilt

STARRY PINWHEELS

The finished size is 28" x 28". The block size is 6".

Refer to quilt drawing and photo for color placement.

SUPPLIES

Blues, Reds, and Yellows for Pinwheels
¼ yard total
(or you could choose one blue, one red, and one yellow, and buy ⅛ yard of each)

Several Black and Muslin Fabrics for Background
¼ yard total

First Border
¼ yard

Second Border
⅛ yard

Third Border and Binding
½ yard

Backing
1 yard

Batting 32" x 32"

CUTTING

Pinwheels: Cut one strip 3⅞" x 42" of each color (red, yellow, blue, black, and muslin). Open the strips and stack them in groups of three and two. Cut 8 squares 3⅞" x 3⅞" of each color. Cut the squares in half diagonally. (*Optional:* Cut individual squares 3⅞" x 3⅞" of several fabrics totaling 36 squares. Cut in half diagonally.)

First Border: Cut two strips 2¼" x 42". Open the strips and stack them. From these strips cut two strips 18½" for the sides; cut two strips 22" for the top and bottom.

Second Border: Cut three strips 1" x 42". Join into one long strip. From these strips cut two strips 22" for the sides; cut two strips 23" for top and bottom.

Third Border: Cut three strips 3" x 42". Join into one long strip. From this strip cut two strips 23" for the sides; cut two strips 28" for the top and bottom.
Binding: Cut three strips 1¼" x 42". Join into one long strip. From this strip cut two strips 28" for the sides; cut two strips 28½" for the top and bottom.

Backing: Cut one piece 32" x 32".

❖ *A quilt with a varied collection of fabrics needs a strong border to frame and contain it. I used the black first, then narrow yellow for an accent (a little goes a long way) and finally the red stars. When it was bordered, the quilt seemed to have an Americana or folk art look.*

Sewing instructions begin on next page.

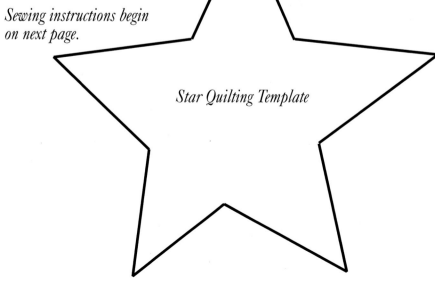

Star Quilting Template

SEWING INSTRUCTIONS FOR STARRY PINWHEELS

Review the Quilting Basics in Chapter 2 before you begin.

1. If you are aiming for a collected fabric look for the Pinwheels, arrange the fabrics into nine blocks on a flannel wall to plan the quilt (see box). Sew two half-square triangles together to make up a quarter of one block, then join these into rows. Stitch row 1 to row 2, etc. (If you are using just three fabrics, then follow the instructions on page 57 for basic block construction.) Make nine blocks.

2. Follow the straight set instructions on page 33 for sewing the blocks together.

3. Follow the instructions on page 33 for adding borders.

4. Follow the instructions on page 35 for basting the quilt.

5. The Pinwheel blocks were hand-quilted ¼" away from each seam. The star template on page 63 was placed randomly on the borders, traced, and hand-quilted.

6. Follow the instructions on page 37 for binding the quilt.

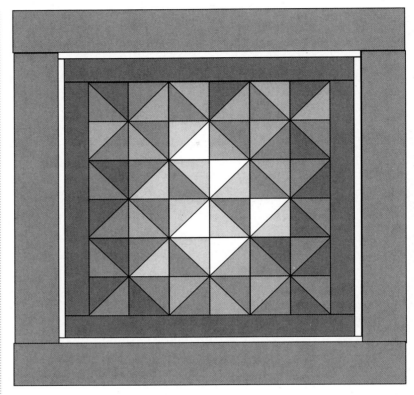

Starry Pinwheels Quilt Drawing

❖ *When I begin to put colors together for a quilt like this, I put a piece of flannel or batting (something that fabric will stick to) on a wall. Then I cut out lots of the Pinwheel sections and start placing them on the flannel. If you have a high contrast color like the yellow, remember that the eye will be drawn to it. Use it sparingly and remember that the specific placement is important. I concentrated it in the center. Another idea would be to scatter it across the quilt from the top left to the bottom right. Remember that the eye will follow it.*

AMISH PINWHEELS

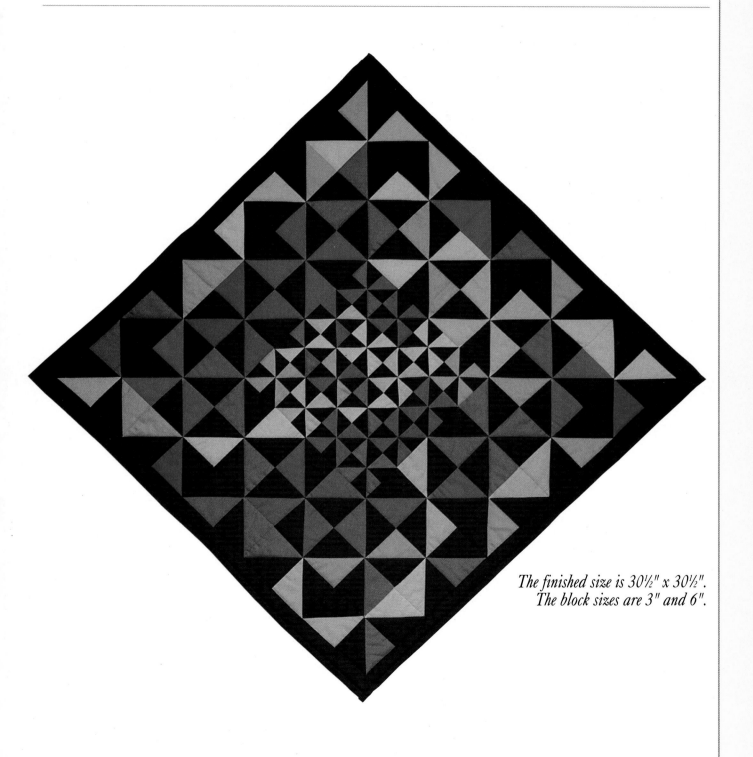

The finished size is 30½" x 30½".
The block sizes are 3" and 6".

Refer to quilt drawing and photo for color placement.

SUPPLIES

Pinwheel Blocks
¼ yard each of six colors
(two shades each of
pink, purple and green)

Background
and Binding
1½ yard black

Backing
1 yard

Batting 35" x 35"

CUTTING

3" Pinwheels (center of the quilt): Cut one strip 2⅜" x 42" of each color. Cut six strips of the background (black) 2⅜" x 42". Open the strips and stack them with right sides together of each pair, in stacks of six in this order: black, light pink, black, light green, black, dark purple. Cut this strip stack into five squares 2⅜" x 2⅜". Cut in half diagonally. Make a second stack in this order: black, dark pink, black, light purple, black, dark green. Cut this strip stack into six squares 2⅜" x 2⅜". Cut in half diagonally. (See the box on page 67.)

6" Pinwheels and Pieced Border: You will need 12 Pinwheels for the quilt and 18 half Pinwheels for the border. Cut one strip 3⅞" x 42" of each color and six strips 3⅞" x 42" of the background (black). Repeat the process used for cutting the small Pinwheels, making three stacks of four strips in this order:
Stack #1—black, dark green, black, light purple.
Cut six squares 3⅞" x 3⅞". Cut in half diagonally.
Stack #2—black, light pink, black, light green.
Cut seven squares 3⅞" x 3⅞". Cut in half diagonally.
Stack #3—black, dark pink, black, dark purple.
Cut eight squares 3⅞" x 3⅞". Cut in half diagonally.
(See the box on page 67.)

Binding: Cut four strips 1¾" x 42". From these strips cut two strips 30½" for the sides; cut two strips 31" for the top and bottom.

Backing: Cut one piece 35" x 35".

SEWING INSTRUCTIONS FOR AMISH PINWHEELS

Review the Quilting Basics in Chapter 2 before you begin.

1. Follow the general instructions for Pinwheel block construction on page 57. When you sew the half-square triangles, always have the colored fabric on top and the black on the bottom.

❖ *When making the half-square triangles, you will save time if the black and colored strips are layered and cut together. Then they can be picked up, ready to sew.*

2. For the half-square triangles in the 3" blocks, follow the same steps of pairing each color with black, and make 10 squares each with light pink, dark purple, and light green. Make 11 each dark pink and dark green squares. Make 12 light purple squares.

3. For the half-square triangles in the 6" blocks and the pieced border, make 12 each of light purple and dark green squares. Make 14 each light pink and light green squares. Make 16 each dark pink and dark purple squares.

4. Look at the photo on page 65 to determine the color configuration of each block, or make up your own. Make 16 blocks that are 3" and 12 blocks that are 6". The remaining squares are for the pieced border that is made up of half-square triangle blocks.

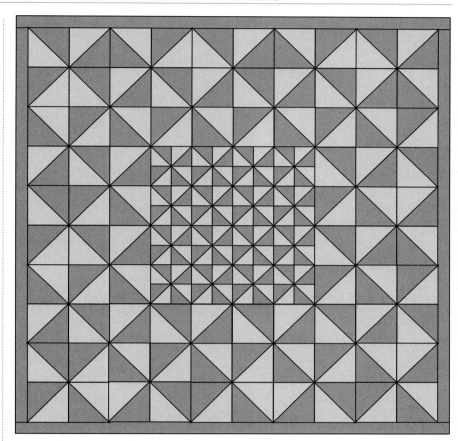

Amish Pinwheels Quilt Drawing

5. Arrange all of the blocks on a bed or table. Follow the straight set instructions on page 33 for sewing the blocks together.

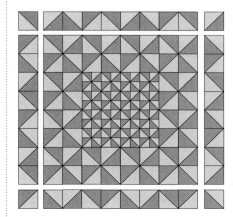

6. To make the pieced outer row, arrange the blocks around the quilt. Sew the half-square triangles into a row for the side borders. Then repeat for the top and bottom, adding corner half-square triangles in a square to each end.

7. Follow the instructions on page 33 for adding the borders.

8. Follow the instructions on page 35 for basting the quilt.

9. This quilt is machine-quilted in-the-ditch.

10. Follow the instructions on page 37 for binding the quilt.

HOUR GLASS PINWHEELS

The finished size is 33½" x 45½". The block size is 6".

Refer to quilt drawing and photo for color placement.

SUPPLIES

Background
1⅛ yards

**First-Color Pinwheels,
Accent Strip, and
Binding**
1⅛ yards

**Second-Color
Pinwheels**
⅝ yards

Backing
1⅜ yards

Batting 38" x 50"

CUTTING

Pinwheels: Cut seven strips 3⅞" x 42" from the background.
For Pinwheel colors, cut three and one-half strips 3⅞" x 42" of each color.
Open the strips and stack them with right sides together for each pair
in stacks of four (background, first color, background, second color).
Cut into a total of 140 squares 3⅞" x 3⅞". Cut in half diagonally.
(Leave these stacked and ready to sew.)
Border Pinwheels: Cut three strips 2⅜" x 42" from background.
From Pinwheel colors, cut one and one-half strips 2⅜" x 42" of each color.
Follow directions above in stacking and cutting a total of
100 squares 2⅜" x 2⅜". Cut in half diagonally.
Accent Strip: Cut four strips 1" x 42". Join into one long strip.
From this strip cut two strips 42½" for the sides; cut two strips 30½"
for the top and bottom.
Binding: Cut four strips 1¾" x 42". Join into one long strip.
From this strip cut two strips 45½" for the sides; cut two strips 34"
for the top and bottom.

Backing: Cut one piece 38" x 50".

SEWING INSTRUCTIONS FOR HOUR GLASS PINWHEELS

*Review the Quilting Basics in
Chapter 2 before you begin.*

1. Follow the block instructions on
page 57 and complete 35 Pinwheel
blocks for the top.

2. Arrange them in a pleasing order.
Follow the straight set instructions
on page 33 for sewing the blocks
together. Follow directions in box
at right to add the accent strip.

3. Complete 100 half-square
triangles for the border. Stitch 28
units together for each side, and
add these to the quilt. Stitch 22
together for the top and bottom,
and add these to the quilt.

4. Follow the instructions on
page 35 for basting the quilt.

5. This quilt was machine-quilted
in-the-ditch on all seams.

6. Follow the instructions on
page 37 for binding the quilt.

*Hour Glass Pinwheels
Quilt Drawing*

❖ *To create an accent in the
border seam, cut a 1" strip of
fabric in a high-contrast color.
Fold it in half lengthwise and
press it. Insert it into the seam
by laying it on the edge of the
quilt with raw edges even
before you attach the border
strip. These border accents
(or unstuffed piping) will
overlap at the corners.*

Chapter Five

SAWTOOTH STAR QUILTS

CHAPTER FIVE

Sawtooth Star Quilts

Sawtooth Stars are some of my favorite quilts to make, probably because they are easy and there are so many variations possible. Stars denote special occasions like the Fourth of July, a romantic evening sky, or a famous person. As you can see from the quilts shown, the stars can be single fabrics or a variety of fabrics. Lawry Thorn, my store manager, teaches a Star Sampler class, and it is one of the most popular classes, testimony to the enduring appeal of stars.

Stars Above is a medallion quilt that Lawry made. The center of the quilt is a 6" star. The 6" star then becomes the center block of the 12" star. The unit in the blocks that makes the star points can be repeated alone. In this quilt, those star points become a border of the "Flying Geese" design with the final border made from small Sawtooth Stars. For a background fabric she chose a large muted print in a light value. By using the same fabric for the background throughout, it gave the design consistency. In the beginning the burgundy was going to be the accent color, but the light pink really made it sing.

The design in *Sawtooth Garden* incorporates an interesting sashing technique. The solid-colored stars are created at the intersection where the sashing meets between the blocks in this diagonal block setting. The star point unit is added to each end of the sashing where it meets the corner post. I like the effect it gives, especially in the diagonal setting.

Primarily Stars is such a bright, graphic quilt, and it is easy. The colors for the stars come from the background print. I like the yellow-green and yellow-gold as a change from the typical primary-secondary colors. The pieced border is an effective way to use leftovers and repeat the star colors all at the same time. I use this technique a lot to repeat the quilt colors in the border and give the quilt unity.

Ursula Searles created *Sawtooth Trail*. She is an expert scrap-quilt maker. The consistent elements here are a tan background, black star points, and red and black squares that trail across the quilt. Look closely at the variety of fabrics that she used. There are tomato reds, true reds, maroon— and they all work.

Both *Sawtooth Trail* on page 75 and *Stars Above* on page 83 are scrap quilts. This means a variety of fabrics are used in each color group in the quilt. Successful scrap quilts still need to have a theme. Use lights or darks in the same position throughout the quilt blocks. I like to combine various styles of fabric, as you can see in *Stars Above*, but keep the background in all of the blocks consistent.

SAWTOOTH STAR BLOCK INSTRUCTIONS

Another step on the path to easy quiltmaking sets you down in a sky filled with bright and beautiful Sawtooth Stars!
Read through all of the general instructions before you begin these projects.

Double Half-Square Triangles

This unit looks like two half-square triangles joined at the center, but there is no seam. There are several methods for making this unit. The method below is easy for beginners to keep the seam straight. It involves stitching folded square units to the ends of a rectangular unit and then trimming.

1. Fold B in half diagonally and lightly press the fold. Unfold the square. You will need eight of these for each Sawtooth Star block.

2. Place the right side of B onto a short end of C and sew along the fold line diagonally across the square.

3. Trim away excess fabric leaving a ¼" seam allowance.

4. Open the triangle and press toward B.

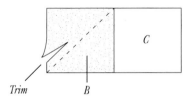

5. Repeat for the other side of the triangle.

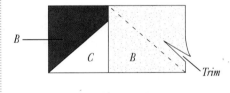

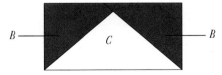

This unit by itself is called Flying Geese. You see it in the border of *Stars Above*.

BLOCK INSTRUCTIONS

Constructing the Sawtooth Star Block

The Sawtooth Star block has two shapes: squares and star points. You can see the large square in the center of the block and four smaller squares in the corners. The star points are separate units called double half-square triangles. There are four of these.

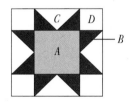

1. Construct the BC units first, referring to the Double Half-Square Triangle section on page 73 to complete four units.

2. Lay out all of the sections of the block and construct in the following rows:

Row 1—Sew patch D to a BC unit, then add another patch D. Press seams toward D.

Row 2—Sew a BC unit to patch A, then add another BC unit. Press seams toward A.

Row 3—Sew patch D to a BC unit, then add another patch D. Press seams toward D.

3. Join Row 1 to Row 2, and then Row 2 to Row 3. Press seams toward Row 2.

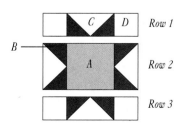

Constructing the Puss in the Corner Block

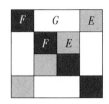

This block consists of squares and rectangles. The center is a Four Patch block. It is bordered with strips and a square in each corner. The series of squares creates a diagonal line across the block.

1. Construct the center Four Patch first. Stitch E and F squares together for Center Row 1, repeat for Center Row 2. Press seam allowances toward the darker color, so the seams will nest together.

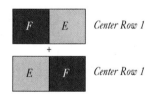

Center Row 1

Center Row 1

Nesting

2. Lay out all of the sections of the block and construct in the following rows:

Row 1—Sew patch F to patch G, then add a patch E of the first color. Press seams toward patch G.

Row 2—Sew patch G to the Four Patch, then add another G. Press seams toward G.

Row 3—Sew patch E to patch G, then add a patch F of the second color. Press seams toward patch G.

3. Join Row 1 to Row 2, and then to Row 3, positioning the different colors of the EF blocks to align diagonally within the block. Press toward Rows 1 and 3.

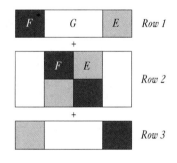

SAWTOOTH TRAIL

The finished size is 76½" x 92½". The block size is 8".

Refer to quilt drawing and photo for color placement.

SUPPLIES

Red Prints
1¾ yards

Black Prints
2¾ yards

Tan Prints
(background)
4¼ yards

Border and Binding
1⅛ yards

Backing 5½ yards

Batting 81" x 97"

CUTTING

Patch A for Star Blocks: Cut six strips 4½" x 42" strips.
Cut into 50 squares 4½" x 4½".
Patch E for Puss in the Corner Blocks: Cut 12½ strips 2½" x 42".
Cut into 196 squares 2½" x 2½".

Patch B for Star Blocks: Cut 25 strips 2½" x 42". Cut into 400 squares 2½" x 2½". Fold the squares in half diagonally and press.
Patch F for Puss in the Corner Blocks: Cut 13 strips 2½" x 42".
Cut into 196 squares 2½" x 2½".

Patch C for Star Blocks: Cut 23 strips 2½" x 42".
Cut into 200 rectangles 2½" x 4½".
Patch D for Star Blocks: Cut 13 strips 2½" x 42".
Cut into 200 squares 2½" x 2½".
Patch G for Puss in the Corner Blocks: Cut 22 strips 2½" x 42".
Cut into 196 rectangles 2½" x 4½".

Border: Cut eight strips 2½" x 42". Join into one long strip.
From this strip cut two strips 88½" for the sides; cut two strips 76½" for the top and bottom.
Binding: Cut nine strips 1¾" x 42". Join into one long strip.
From this strip cut two strips 92½" for the sides; cut two strips 77" for the top and bottom.

Backing: Cut two pieces 97" x 42". Trim off the selvages and sew sections together, right sides facing, along the lengthwise grain.

SEWING INSTRUCTIONS FOR SAWTOOTH TRAIL

Review the Quilting Basics in Chapter 2 before you begin.

1. Follow the block construction instructions on pages 73-74 to make 50 Sawtooth Star and 49 Puss in the Corner blocks.

2. Arrange the blocks as shown in the photograph. Follow the straight set instructions on page 33 for sewing the blocks together.

3. Follow the instructions on page 33 for adding borders.

4. Follow the instructions on page 35 for basting the quilt.

5. This quilt was machine-quilted diagonally across the Sawtooth Stars and the Puss in the Corner blocks.

6. Follow the instructions on page 37 for binding the quilt.

Sawtooth Trail Quilt Drawing

SAWTOOTH GARDEN

The finished size is 54" x 77". The block sizes are 8" and 12".

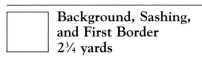

Refer to quilt drawing and photo for color placement.

SUPPLIES

CUTTING

Third Border, Binding, Backing, and Large Star
4½ yards

Large Floral Prints
1¼ yards total or ¼ yard each of seven prints

12" Sawtooth Stars (cut eight):
Cut the backing, third border, and binding from floral fabric first, then use the remainder for large Sawtooth Star blocks. Instructions are given for cutting single stars although you will need a total of eight blocks. You may wish to stack your fabric and cut several at a time.
Third Border: Cut six strips 4½" x 42". Join into one long strip. From this strip cut two strips 69" for sides; cut two strips 54" for the top and bottom.
Binding: Cut seven strips 1¼" x 42". Join into one long strip. From this strip cut two strips 77" for sides; cut two strips 54½" for the top and bottom.
Backing: Cut two pieces 58" x 42". Trim off the selvages and sew sections together, right sides facing, along the lengthwise grain.
Patch A: Cut one square 6½" x 6½".
Patch B: Cut one strip 3½" x 29" strip. From this strip cut eight squares 3½" x 3½". Fold the squares in half diagonally and press along the fold.

Lavender and Pink Solids
⅓ yard of each

8" Sawtooth Stars:
From Lavender, cut four Sawtooth Stars.
Patch A: Cut one strip 4½" x 19".
Cut into four squares 4½" x 4½" (called corner posts).
Patch B: Cut two strips 2½" x 42". Cut strips into 32 squares 2½" x 2½".
Fold the squares in half diagonally and press along the fold.
From pink, cut three Sawtooth Stars.
Patch A: Cut one strip 4½" x 15" strip.
Cut strip into three squares 4½" x 4½" (called corner posts).
Patch B: Cut two strips 2½" x 42". Cut strips into 24 squares 2½" x 2½".
Fold the squares in half diagonally and press along the fold.

Background, Sashing, and First Border
2¾ yards

12" Star Backgrounds:
Patch C: Cut six strips 3½" x 42". Cut into 32 rectangles 3½" x 6½".
Patch D: Cut three strips 3½" x 42". Cut into 32 squares 3½" x 3½".
8" Star Backgrounds:
Patch C: Cut three strips 2½" x 42" and one more rectangle 2½" x 4½".
Cut strips into 28 rectangles 2½" x 4½".
Sashes: Cut five strips 4½" x 42". From these strips cut eight strips 4½" x 8½" and 12 strips 4½" x 10½".
Setting Triangles: Cut two squares 12⅝" x 12⅝".
Cut the squares into quarters diagonally.
Corner Triangles: Cut two squares 9½" x 9½".
Cut the squares in half diagonally.
First Border: Cut five strips 2½" x 42". Join into one long strip.
From this strip cut two strips 63" for sides; cut two strips 44" for top and bottom.

Second Border
⅓ yard

Second Border: Cut six strips 1½" x 42". Join into one long strip. From this strip cut two strips 67" for the sides; cut two strips 46" for the top and bottom.

Batting 58" x 81"

SEWING INSTRUCTIONS FOR SAWTOOTH GARDEN

Review the Quilting Basics in Chapter 2 before you begin.

1. Follow the block construction instructions on page 74 to make eight 12" Sawtooth Star blocks.

2. Refer to the instructions for double half-square triangles on page 73, and construct 16 lavender BC units for the 8" Sawtooth Stars and 12 pink BC units for the 8" Sawtooth Stars. Piece one of each color to the ends of the eight 8½" sashing strips. Piece 8 lavender BC units to eight 10½" sashing strips. Piece 4 pink BC units to four 10½" sashing strips.

3. Arrange the blocks as shown in the photograph, laying out the blocks with the sashing and corner posts, and inserting the setting and corner triangles. Follow the diagonal set instructions on page 33 for sewing the blocks together. Trim 10½" sashing strips even with edge of quilt.

4. Follow the instructions on page 33 for adding borders.

Sawtooth Garden Quilt Drawing

5. Follow the instructions on pages 35 for basting the quilt.

6. This quilt was machine-quilted on the seam lines and on the border. To quilt the border, choose a quilting design that you like, trace it on the border, and quilt.

7. Follow the instructions on page 37 for binding the quilt.

PRIMARILY STARS

The finished size is 40½" x 40½". The block size is 8".

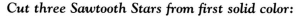

Refer to quilt drawing and photo for color placement.

SUPPLIES

**Four Solid Colors
for Stars and
Second Pieced Border**
⅜ **yard each**

**Dark Print for Star
Backgrounds, Sashes,
First and Third Borders,
Binding, and Backing**
3 yards

Batting 44" x 44"

CUTTING

Cut three Sawtooth Stars from first solid color:
Patch A: Cut one strip 4½" x 15". Cut into three squares 4½" x 4½".
Patch B: Cut two strips 2½" x 42". Cut into 24 squares 2½" x 2½".
Fold the squares in half diagonally and press along the fold.
Cut two Sawtooth Stars from each of the three remaining colors:
(You may wish to stack the fabrics and cut several patches at a time.)
Patch A: Cut one strip 4½" x 10". Cut into two squares 4½" x 4½".
Patch B: Cut one strip 2½" x 42". Cut into 16 squares 2½" x 2½".
Fold the squares in half diagonally and press along the fold.
Second Pieced Border: Cut scraps of the four solid-colored fabrics into strips that are 1½" wide. The length of the pieces can vary from 3" to 4½". Join into one long strip measuring 136". From this strip cut two strips 32½" for the sides; cut two strips 34½" for the top and bottom.

Star Backgrounds:
Patch C: Cut four strips 2½" x 42". Cut into 36 rectangles 2½" x 4½".
Patch D: Cut three strips 2½" x 42". Cut into 36 squares 2½" x 2½".
Sashes: Cut three strips 2½" x 42". From two of the strips cut a strip 2½" x 28½" and a rectangle 2½" x 8½" (for a total of two each). From the remaining 2½" x 42" strip cut four rectangles 2½" x 8½".
First Border: Cut three strips 2½" x 42". Join into one long strip. From this strip cut two strips 28½" for the sides; cut two strips 32½" for the top and bottom.
Third Border: Cut four strips 3½" x 42". From these strips cut two strips 34½" for the sides; cut two strips 40½" for the top and bottom.
Backing: Cut one 42" x 44" piece.
Binding: Cut four strips 1¾" x 42". From these strips cut two strips 40½" for the sides; cut two strips 41" for the top and bottom.

Sewing instructions begin on next page.

SEWING INSTRUCTIONS FOR PRIMARILY STARS

Review the Quilting Basics in Chapter 2 before you begin.

1. Follow the block construction instructions on page 74 to make the nine Sawtooth Star blocks.

2. Arrange the blocks as shown in the photograph, inserting the sashing between them. Follow the straight set instructions on page 33 for sewing the blocks together.

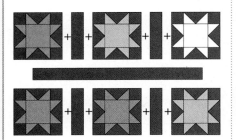

3. Follow the instructions on page 33 to complete the first, second (pieced), and third borders.

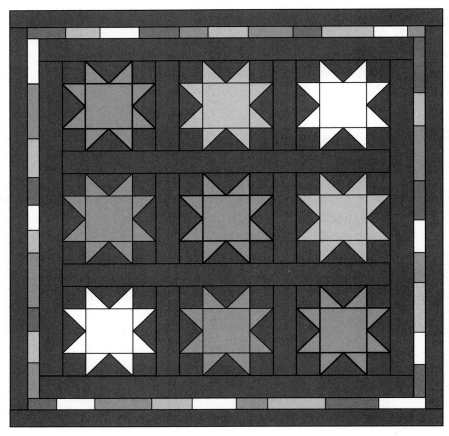

Primarily Stars Quilt Drawing

4. Follow the instructions on pages 35 for basting the quilt.

5. This quilt was machine-quilted in-the-ditch along the major seam lines.

6. Follow the instructions on page 37 for binding the quilt.

STARS ABOVE

The finished size is 28½" x 28½". The block sizes are 4", 6", and 12".

Refer to quilt drawing and photo for color placement.

SUPPLIES	CUTTING

 Large-Theme Print for Center Stars ⅜ yard

Patch B for 12" Sawtooth Star: Cut one strip 3½" x 29".
Cut into eight squares 3½" x 3½". Fold the squares in half diagonally and press along the fold.
Patch C for 6" Sawtooth Star: Cut one strip 2" x 15".
Cut into four rectangles 2" x 3½".
Patch D for 6" Sawtooth Star: Cut one strip 2" x 11".
Cut into four squares 2" x 2".

 Background 1 yard

Patch A for 6" Sawtooth Star: Cut one square 3½" x 3½".
Patch B for 6" Sawtooth Star: Cut one strip 2" x 17".
Cut into eight squares 2" x 2". Fold the squares in half diagonally and press along the fold.
Patch A for 12" Sawtooth Star: Use the 6" Sawtooth Star.
Patch C for 12" Sawtooth Star: Cut one strip 3½" x 27".
Cut into four rectangles 3½" x 6½".
Patch C for 4" Sawtooth Star: Cut one strip 1½" x 11".
Cut into four rectangles 1½ " x 2½". Repeat for 24 Stars.
Patch D for 4" Sawtooth Star: Cut one strip 1½" x 7".
Cut into four squares 1½" x 1½". Repeat for 24 Stars.
Patch B for Flying Geese Border: Cut five strips 2" x 42".
Cut into squares 2" x 2" until you have a total of 88.
Fold the squares in half diagonally and press along the fold.

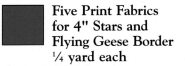 **Five Print Fabrics for 4" Stars and Flying Geese Border** ¼ yard each

Patch C for Flying Geese Border: Cut one strip 2" x 42" from each print fabric. Open strips and stack them. Cut into 44 rectangles 2" x 3½". (Consider how many you want of each color.)
Patch A for 4" Sawtooth Stars: Cut one square 2½" x 2½". Repeat for 24 Stars.
Patch B for 4" Sawtooth Stars: Cut one strip 1½" x 13".
Cut into eight squares 1½" x 1½". Fold the squares in half diagonally and press along the fold. Repeat for 24 Stars.

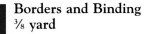 **Borders and Binding** ⅜ yard

First Border: Cut two strips 1¼" x 42". Open the strips and stack them. From these strips cut two strips 12½" for the sides; cut two strips 14" for the top and bottom.
Third Border: Cut two strips ¾" x 42". Open the strips and stack them. From these strips cut two strips 20" for the sides; cut two strips 20½" for the top and bottom.
Binding: Cut three strips 1¼" x 42". Join into one long strip. From this strip cut two strips 28½" for the sides; cut two strips 29" for the top and bottom.

Backing 1 yard

Backing: Cut one piece 33" x 33".

Batting 33" x 33"

SEWING INSTRUCTIONS FOR STARS ABOVE

Review the Quilting Basics in Chapter 2 before you begin.

1. Follow the block construction instructions on page 74 to complete one 6" within a 12" Sawtooth Star and 24 small 4" ones along with 44 Flying Geese blocks.

2. Add the first border to the center block (12" Star) as shown on page 33.

3. Sew nine Flying Geese units together in a row with the points facing right and add to the top of the quilt.

First Border

Flying Geese Border

4. Complete the other three Flying Geese borders as shown and add to the remaining sides of the quilt.

5. Add the third border to the quilt as shown on page 33.

6. Sew two rows of five Sawtooth Stars together, then sew to the sides of the quilt. Sew two rows of seven Sawtooth Stars together and add to the top and bottom of the quilt.

Stars Above Quilt Drawing

Third Border

7. Follow the instructions on page 35 for basting the quilt.

8. This quilt is machine-quilted along the seam lines of the center Star, along the edge of each border, and between each block on the outer border.

9. Follow the instructions on page 37 for binding the quilt.

85

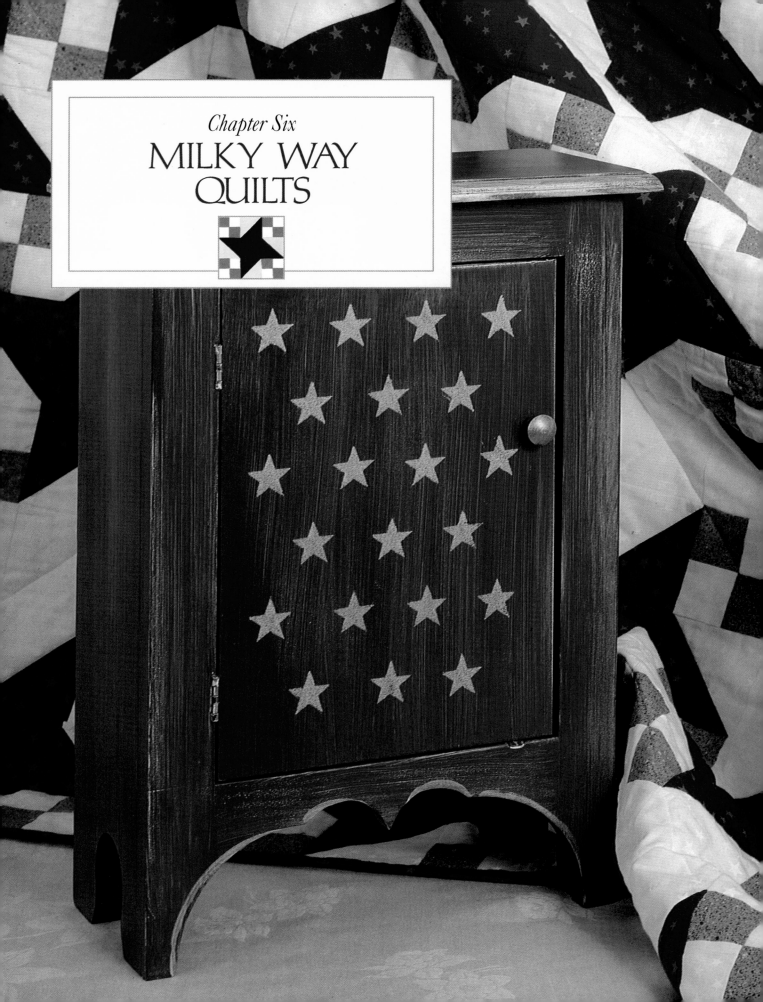

Chapter Six
MILKY WAY QUILTS

CHAPTER SIX

Milky Way Quilts

I discovered the Milky Way block in a very old patchwork publication. The block design is based on an interlocking star, as you can see from the quilts. The appearance of the stars reflects a feeling of our galaxy in most of the quilts. The Four Patch units in the block add another dimension that changes with the use of colors in the quilts. *Tessellating Stars* omits the Four Patch entirely so you just see interlocking stars.

The star points in the block are simple half-square triangles that angle out from the center. This simple block is reduced to a smaller version and used for a border in *Christmas Village* on page 221. You will discover even more variations as you work on this block.

When you view these quilts you will see two star patterns emerge, a lighter version and a darker one. In the *Galaxy* quilt pictured on page 94, the light blue squares hook onto the tips of the star points to create a snail effect. This quilt has no border. Many of the antique quilts didn't. You could easily add one if you want to frame it.

Twilight Stars uses a very dark fabric with a light one for the stars. The Four Patch units in the blocks are of a medium value. When viewed from a distance the light gray stars are more dominant.

One night at the Mt. Bachelor Quilters' meeting show-and-tell in Bend, Oregon, Nancy Gray, Victoria Brady, and Sandi Abernathy all stood up together with Milky Way quilts. I was thrilled to see what they had done. Nancy's quilt is *Star Gardens* on page 92. She has used a packed-together floral for the theme fabric and extracted her other colors from it.

The three women agreed to design a quilt for the book. *Tessellating Stars* is the end result. The quilt incorporates several different colors for the stars and omits the Four Patch. The background fabric is the theme fabric with the solid colors dancing around the quilt.

MILKY WAY BLOCK INSTRUCTIONS

The Milky Way is filled with interlocking stars that shimmer and glow along your easy quiltmaking path.
Read through all of the general instructions before you begin these projects.

The Milky Way block has an interlocking star effect when it is repeated. Look at the illustration below and isolate one star in the left-hand corner of the drawing. Then look down to the second star. You will see that the background color in the first block becomes the star point of the second block. Keep following the rows and you will see where row five in the piecing is the same as row one at the top where you started.

When I am ready to assemble this quilt, I lay out the individual units in rows so I can make sure that I haven't twisted a unit around. This will also make the row construction much easier.

The block consists of three units. Unit 1 is a Four Patch (four squares sewn together). Unit 2 is two half-square triangles that make a square. Unit 3 is a square. All of the units are the same size, and it takes nine units to create the star block.

Unit 1

1. To make Unit 1, sew two strips of equal width together. Press the seams toward the darker strip.

Cut

2. Cut across the two strips as shown. The width of the cut will be the same width as the strips that make up the unit. For example, if you begin with a 2½" strip, the width of the cut will be 2½".

3. To construct the unit, place two sets of blocks together, alternating the dark and light to create a checkerboard effect. Place right sides of the sets of units together. The seams will automatically nest together. Stitch. Press seam allowances in one direction. Make four of these units for each Milky Way block.

Unit 1

Unit 2

1. Pick up a pair of half-square triangles (star fabric and background fabric) and put right sides together. Always keep the same color of fabric on top. Stitch pairs together along the longest side.

2. Feed pairs of triangles through the sewing machine, one after the other without lifting the presser foot. There will be a small chain of stitches between the units, creating a string of stitched units.

3. Remove the chain of stitched units from the machine. Clip the threads between the pairs to release them. Press both seam allowances toward the darker of the two fabrics.

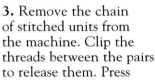
Trim
Trim

4. Trim off the excess seam allowances even with the edge of the unit. Make four of these units for each Milky Way block.

Unit 3

This unit is a square in the center of the star. Cut one of these square units for each Milky Way block.

Once all the units are completed for the block, lay them out on your work surface. Stitch the three units in each row together, then sew one row to the next until all three rows are stitched together to complete a block.

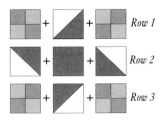
Row 1
Row 2
Row 3

TWILIGHT STARS

The finished size is 57½" x 73½". Block size is 12" with a 4" unit repeat.

Refer to quilt drawing and photo for color placement.

SUPPLIES

 Dark Stars, Second Border, and Binding
2¼ yards

 Light Stars
1¼ yards

 Medium Blue Print for Four Patch
½ yard

 Red Print for Four Patch and First Border
1⅛ yards

Backing
3½ yards

Batting 62" x 78"

CUTTING

Dark and Light Stars (Patch B): Cut six strips 4⅞" x 42" of each color. Open the strips and stack them with right sides together, in each of the pairs (one dark, one light), in stacks of four. Cut into 41 squares 4⅞" x 4⅞" of each color. Cut the squares in half diagonally.

Star Centers (Patch C): Cut two strips 4½" x 42" of each color. Open the strips and stack them. Cut 18 dark and 17 light squares 4½" x 4½".

Second Border: Cut six strips 4" x 42" of the dark color. Join into one long strip. From this strip cut two strips 66½" for the sides; cut two strips 57½" for the top and bottom.

Binding: Cut seven strips 1¾" x 42". Join into one long strip. From this strip cut two strips 73½" for the sides; cut two strips 58" for the top and bottom.

Four Patches (Patch A): Cut six strips of each color, 2½" x 42".

First Border: Cut six strips 3½" x 42". Join into one long strip. From this strip cut two strips 60½" for the sides; cut two strips 50½" for the top and bottom.

Backing: Cut two pieces 62" x 42". Trim off the selvages and sew sections together, right sides facing, along the lengthwise grain.

SEWING INSTRUCTIONS FOR TWILIGHT STARS

Review the Quilting Basics in Chapter 2 before you begin.

1. To make the Four Patch (Unit 1), refer to the general instructions on page 89. Cut the strips at 2½" intervals (96 total). Sew into 48 Four Patches.

2. To make the half-square triangle square (Unit 2), refer to page 89. Make 82 pieced squares.

3. Following the quilt drawing, lay out the units and Star Centers. Follow the straight set instructions on page 33 for sewing the blocks together.

4. Follow the instructions on page 33 for adding the borders.

5. Follow the instructions on page 35 for basting the quilt.

6. This quilt is machine-quilted along the edges of the Stars in-the-ditch and along the edge of each border.

7. Follow the instructions on page 37 for binding the quilt.

Twilight Stars Quilt Drawing

STAR GARDENS

The finished size is 54" x 70". The block size is 12" with a 4" unit repeat.

MILKY WAY BLOCK INSTRUCTIONS

The Milky Way is filled with interlocking stars that shimmer and glow along your easy quiltmaking path.
Read through all of the general instructions before you begin these projects.

The Milky Way block has an interlocking star effect when it is repeated. Look at the illustration below and isolate one star in the left-hand corner of the drawing. Then look down to the second star. You will see that the background color in the first block becomes the star point of the second block. Keep following the rows and you will see where row five in the piecing is the same as row one at the top where you started.

When I am ready to assemble this quilt, I lay out the individual units in rows so I can make sure that I haven't twisted a unit around. This will also make the row construction much easier.

The block consists of three units. Unit 1 is a Four Patch (four squares sewn together). Unit 2 is two half-square triangles that make a square. Unit 3 is a square. All of the units are the same size, and it takes nine units to create the star block.

Unit 1

1. To make Unit 1, sew two strips of equal width together. Press the seams toward the darker strip.

Cut

2. Cut across the two strips as shown. The width of the cut will be the same width as the strips that make up the unit. For example, if you begin with a 2½" strip, the width of the cut will be 2½".

3. To construct the unit, place two sets of blocks together, alternating the dark and light to create a checkerboard effect. Place right sides of the sets of units together. The seams will automatically nest together. Stitch. Press seam allowances in one direction. Make four of these units for each Milky Way block.

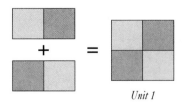

Unit 1

Unit 2

1. Pick up a pair of half-square triangles (star fabric and background fabric) and put right sides together. Always keep the same color of fabric on top. Stitch pairs together along the longest side.

2. Feed pairs of triangles through the sewing machine, one after the other without lifting the presser foot. There will be a small chain of stitches between the units, creating a string of stitched units.

3. Remove the chain of stitched units from the machine. Clip the threads between the pairs to release them. Press both seam allowances toward the darker of the two fabrics.

Trim
Trim

4. Trim off the excess seam allowances even with the edge of the unit. Make four of these units for each Milky Way block.

Unit 3

This unit is a square in the center of the star. Cut one of these square units for each Milky Way block.

Once all the units are completed for the block, lay them out on your work surface. Stitch the three units in each row together, then sew one row to the next until all three rows are stitched together to complete a block.

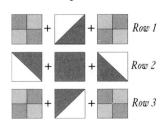

Row 1
Row 2
Row 3

TWILIGHT STARS

The finished size is 57½" x 73½". Block size is 12" with a 4" unit repeat.

Refer to quilt drawing and photo for color placement.

SUPPLIES

Dark Stars, Second Border, and Binding
2¼ yards

Light Stars
1¼ yards

Medium Blue Print for Four Patch
½ yard

Red Print for Four Patch and First Border
1⅛ yards

Backing
3½ yards

Batting 62" x 78"

CUTTING

Dark and Light Stars (Patch B): Cut six strips 4⅞" x 42" of each color. Open the strips and stack them with right sides together, in each of the pairs (one dark, one light), in stacks of four. Cut into 41 squares 4⅞" x 4⅞" of each color. Cut the squares in half diagonally.

Star Centers (Patch C): Cut two strips 4½" x 42" of each color. Open the strips and stack them. Cut 18 dark and 17 light squares 4½" x 4½".

Second Border: Cut six strips 4" x 42" of the dark color. Join into one long strip. From this strip cut two strips 66½" for the sides; cut two strips 57½" for the top and bottom.

Binding: Cut seven strips 1¾" x 42". Join into one long strip. From this strip cut two strips 73½" for the sides; cut two strips 58" for the top and bottom.

Four Patches (Patch A): Cut six strips of each color, 2½" x 42".

First Border: Cut six strips 3½" x 42". Join into one long strip. From this strip cut two strips 60½" for the sides; cut two strips 50½" for the top and bottom.

Backing: Cut two pieces 62" x 42". Trim off the selvages and sew sections together, right sides facing, along the lengthwise grain.

SEWING INSTRUCTIONS FOR TWILIGHT STARS

Review the Quilting Basics in Chapter 2 before you begin.

1. To make the Four Patch (Unit 1), refer to the general instructions on page 89. Cut the strips at 2½" intervals (96 total). Sew into 48 Four Patches.

2. To make the half-square triangle square (Unit 2), refer to page 89. Make 82 pieced squares.

3. Following the quilt drawing, lay out the units and Star Centers. Follow the straight set instructions on page 33 for sewing the blocks together.

4. Follow the instructions on page 33 for adding the borders.

5. Follow the instructions on page 35 for basting the quilt.

6. This quilt is machine-quilted along the edges of the Stars in-the-ditch and along the edge of each border.

7. Follow the instructions on page 37 for binding the quilt.

Twilight Stars Quilt Drawing

STAR GARDENS

The finished size is 54" x 70". The block size is 12" with a 4" unit repeat.

Refer to quilt drawing and photo for color placement.

SUPPLIES

Purple Print for Stars and First Border
1½ yards

Floral Print for Stars, Second Border, and Binding
2½ yards

Green for Four Patch and Binding
½ yard

Pink for Four Patch
½ yard

Backing
3¼ yards

Batting 58" x 74"

CUTTING

Dark and Light Stars (Patch B): Cut six strips 4⅞" x 42" of each color. Open the strips and stack them with right sides together in each of the pairs (one purple, one floral), in stacks of four. Cut into 41 squares 4⅞" x 4⅞" of each color. Cut in half diagonally.

Star Centers (Patch C): Cut two strips 4½" x 42" of each color. Open the strips and stack them. Cut 18 purple and 17 floral squares 4½" x 4½".

First Border: Cut six strips 1½" x 42". Join into one long strip. From this strip cut two strips 60½" for sides; cut two strips 46½" for the top and bottom.

Second Border: Cut six strips 4¼" x 42" of floral print. Join into one long strip. From this strip cut two strips 62½" for the sides; cut two strips 54" for the top and bottom.

Binding: Cut six strips 1¾" x 42". Join into one long strip. From this strip cut two strips 70" for the sides; cut two strips 54½" for the top and bottom.

Four Patches (Patch A): Cut six strips 2½" x 42" of each color.

Backing: Cut two pieces 58" x 42". Trim off the selvages and sew sections together, right sides facing, along the lengthwise grain.

SEWING INSTRUCTIONS FOR STAR GARDENS

Review the Quilting Basics in Chapter 2 before you begin.

1. To make the Four Patch (Unit 1), refer to the general instructions on page 89. Cut the strips at 2½" intervals (96 total). Sew into 48 Four Patches.

2. To make the half-square triangle square (Unit 2), refer to page 89. Make 82 pieced squares.

3. Following the quilt drawing, lay out the units and and Star Centers. Follow the straight set instructions on page 33 for sewing the blocks together.

4. Follow the instructions on page 33 for adding the borders.

5. Follow the instructions on page 35 for basting the quilt.

6. This quilt is machine-quilted in-the-ditch along all seams of the Stars and Four Patch units. A second line of quilting appears ½" in from the edge of the stars.

7. Follow the instructions on page 37 for binding the quilt.

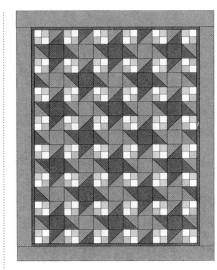

Star Gardens Quilt Drawing

GALAXY

The finished size is 68½" x 84½". The block size is 12" with a 4" unit repeat.

Refer to quilt drawing and photo for color placement.

SUPPLIES	CUTTING

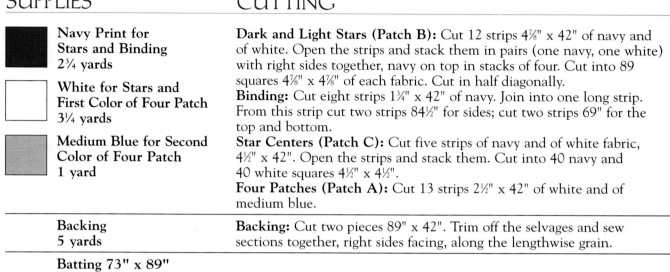

Navy Print for Stars and Binding
2¾ yards

White for Stars and First Color of Four Patch
3¼ yards

Medium Blue for Second Color of Four Patch
1 yard

Dark and Light Stars (Patch B): Cut 12 strips 4⅞" x 42" of navy and of white. Open the strips and stack them in pairs (one navy, one white) with right sides together, navy on top in stacks of four. Cut into 89 squares 4⅞" x 4⅞" of each fabric. Cut in half diagonally.
Binding: Cut eight strips 1¼" x 42" of navy. Join into one long strip. From this strip cut two strips 84½" for sides; cut two strips 69" for the top and bottom.
Star Centers (Patch C): Cut five strips of navy and of white fabric, 4½" x 42". Open the strips and stack them. Cut into 40 navy and 40 white squares 4½" x 4½".
Four Patches (Patch A): Cut 13 strips 2½" x 42" of white and of medium blue.

Backing
5 yards

Backing: Cut two pieces 89" x 42". Trim off the selvages and sew sections together, right sides facing, along the lengthwise grain.

Batting 73" x 89"

Sewing instructions begin on next page.

SEWING INSTRUCTIONS FOR GALAXY

Review the Quilting Basics in Chapter 2 before you begin.

1. To make the Four Patch (Unit 1), refer to the general instructions on page 89. Cut the strips at 2½" intervals (198 total). Sew into 99 Four Patches.

2. To make the half-square triangle square (Unit 2), refer to page 89. Make 178 pieced squares.

3. Following the quilt drawing, lay out the units and the Star Centers. Follow the straight set instructions on page 33 for sewing the blocks together.

4. Follow the instructions on page 35 for basting the quilt.

5. This quilt was machine-quilted. See illustration below for quilting ideas.

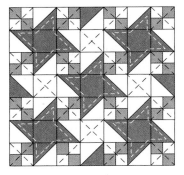

6. Follow the instructions on page 37 for binding the quilt.

Galaxy Quilt Drawing

TESSELLATING STARS

The finished size is 68½" x 68½". The block size is 12" with a 4" repeat.

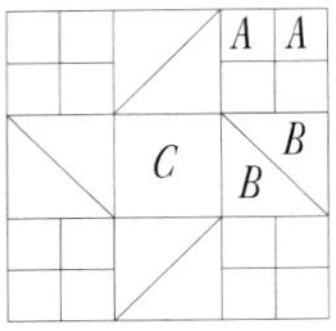

Refer to quilt drawing and photo for color placement. The colors are named starting from any corner for easy reference. Just substitute your color choices.

SUPPLIES

CUTTING

You will need to cut 4½" squares as well as 4⅞" half-square triangles according to the charts below. Both charts use the following fabric key: Bg=background, B=blue, P=pink, L=lavender, R=rose, V=violet, G=green.

Stars
⅝ yard Pink

¾ yard Lavender

¾ yard Rose

½ yard Blue

½ yard Violet

½ yard Green

Background,
Border, Binding
2⅞ yards

Cutting 4½" Squares:

Color:	Strips Needed:	Cut into:
Bg	seven 4½" x 42"	61 squares
B	one 4½" x 22"	4 squares
P	one 4½" x 42"	8 squares
L	two 4½" x 42"	12 squares
R	two 4½" x 42"	16 squares
V	one 4½" x 42"	8 squares
G	one 4½" x 22"	4 squares

Cutting 4⅞" Half-Square Triangles: Cut strips of each color in the length specified. Stack strips in pairs with right sides facing and cut into 4⅞" squares. Then cut the squares in half diagonally.

Color Pairs:	Strips Needed of Each Color:	No. of Squares to Cut of Each Color:	Total Half-Square Triangles of Each Color:
Bg/B	one 4⅞" x 22"	4	8
Bg/P	one 4⅞" x 22"	4	8
Bg/L	one 4⅞" x 22"	4	8
Bg/R	one 4⅞" x 11"	2	4
Bg/G	one 4⅞" x 11"	2	4
B/P	one 4⅞" x 22"	4	8
P/L	one 4⅞" x 42"	8	16
L/R	two 4⅞" x 42"	12	24
R/V	two 4⅞" x 42"	10	20
V/G	one 4⅞" x 42"	6	12

Border: Cut six strips 4½" x 42", and one piece 4½" x 10".
Join into one long strip. From this strip cut two strips 60½" for the sides; cut two strips 68½" for the top and bottom.
Binding: Cut seven strips 1¾" x 42". Join into one long strip.
From this strip cut two strips 68½" for the sides; cut two strips 69" for the top and bottom.

Backing
4 yards

Backing: Cut two lengths 42" x 72". Trim off the selvages and sew sections together, right sides facing, along the lengthwise grain.

Batting 72" x 72"

SEWING INSTRUCTIONS FOR TESSELLATING STARS

Review the Quilting Basics in Chapter 2 before you begin.

1. Follow the cutting chart and prepare all of the half-square triangles to make two-color squares. Basic instructions are on page 89.

2. Look at the photo and arrange the units and the star centers. Follow the straight set instructions on page 33 for sewing the blocks together.

3. Follow the instructions on page 33 for adding the borders.

4. Follow the instructions on page 35 for basting the quilt.

5. This quilt was machine-quilted in-the-ditch. Then the Stars were echo-quilted inside the stars.

6. Follow the instructions on page 37 for binding the quilt.

❖ *In a larger space like a star, once the outline has been quilted then consider "echo quilting." This means that you repeat the star shape every ¼" from the previous line. Repeat this at least three times. It helps to emphasize the shape of the design.*

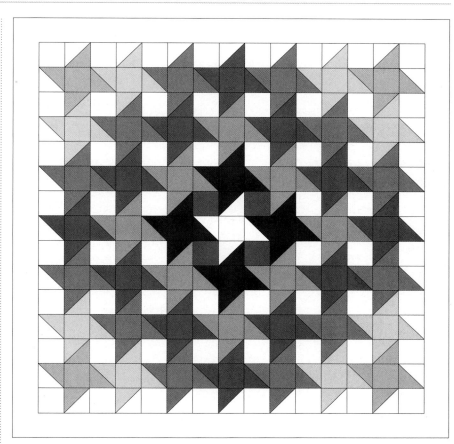

Tessellating Stars Quilt Drawing

CHAPTER SEVEN

Country Bunny Quilts

Rabbits are among my favorite animals. At my house, I have a bathroom decorated with all kinds of rabbits. They are even starting to overflow into the other parts of the house. I like the soft shape of the rabbit in this chapter as it sits with its ears perked up. This shape is at home on a baby quilt, a youth blanket, or perfect for a country-style wall hanging.

The first quilt that I designed for this chapter was *Bunny Melody*, intended for a friend who was having a baby. I picked colors that could be for either a boy or girl. The green is a very neutral color and helps to pull together the other colors. This quilt carries the look of springtime or new beginnings. The design is built around the bunny panel in the center. Pinwheels and checks surround the bunnies and border the quilt.

Bunny Hop is a brighter rendition of the medallion center in *Bunny Melody*. The black really makes the mint green and grape colors pop.

Lately I've been seeing a lot of hand-painted furniture with black-and-white checks. This was the inspiration for *Checkerboard Bunnies*. I wanted to work with all solids and design a quilt that could be used for a toddler. The moon and star appliqués create a story-book mood.

I live in the country and love my wildflower garden, even though I have to share it with the deer. When I saw the large floral print used for the background fabric in *Rabbit Patch*, I just couldn't resist it. It reminds me of fall. The rabbit fabrics are color extractions from the print. Once the rabbit blocks were done, I needed to determine a setting. The little plaid in lighter colors seemed right with the Four Patch accent. This quilt will adorn my kitchen wall some day when I have time to make one for myself.

Garden Variety is a sampling of bright summer flowers and geometrics. Whenever you use a variety of fabrics in a quilt, you should establish a constant element in the design. This will give the quilt unity. In this quilt the bunnies are always a black print and the backgrounds a light floral. The border incorporates both since it is a black stripe over a floral. The pastel Pinwheels add interest like bright flowers in a garden.

BUNNY QUILT BLOCK INSTRUCTIONS

This quiltmaking path has Country Bunnies that frolic and dance. These easy-appliqué bunnies will make you smile. Read through all of the general instructions before you begin these projects.

Most of these Bunny quilts were planned for walls, cribs, or single beds. You may make adjustments in border widths or add more borders. Choose whether you will use machine, hand, or fusible appliqué before you begin. Refer to pages 31-32. Our project instructions are for fusible appliqué.

Block Construction

There are a variety of small units that combine to make The Country Bunny Quilts. The Pinwheel block is explained on page 57. The appliqué techniques are described on pages 31-32. And, finally, the Four Patch and Checkerboard blocks are described here.

1. To make the basic unit for Four Patch and Checkerboard blocks, sew two fabric strips of equal width and length together along the long edge. Press the seam allowances toward the darker strip.

2. Cut across the two strips the width of the single strip with which you started. (If the strip was 2½" x 42", cut across every 2½".) Continue cutting until the entire strip is cut up.

3. To make a Four Patch block, join two pairs, positioning the colors opposite each other.

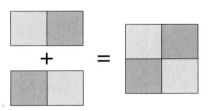

4. To make a Checkerboard border, join pairs, switching the colors each time until it is the length you desire.

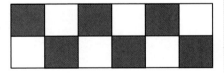

5. To make an alternating square border, join pairs end to end, alternating a light square with a dark square. Repeat light, dark, light, dark, and so forth.

BUNNY MELODY

The finished size is 35" x 48½".

Refer to quilt drawing and photo for color placement.

SUPPLIES

CUTTING

Green Textured Print for Borders and Binding
1 yard

Patch C: Cut two strips 1½" x 42". Open the strips and stack them. From these strips cut two strips 14½" for the sides; cut two strips 24½" for the top and bottom.
Patch H: Cut four strips 4½" x 12".
Patch I: Cut four strips 4½" x 18½".
Binding: Cut five strips 1¼" x 42". Join into one long strip. From this strip cut two strips 48½" for the sides; cut two strips 35½" long for the top and bottom.

Light Green Print for Grass
⅛ yard

Patch A2: Cut one strip 4" x 18½".

Background
⅞ yard

Background A1: Cut one strip 7" x 18½".
Background E: Cut one strip 4½" x 28". Cut into six squares 4½" x 4½".
Background G: Cut two strips 7" x 27½".

Yellow, Lavender, Pink, and Peach Checks and Prints for Bunnies and Hearts
¼ yard each of two different fabrics of each color

Bunnies and Hearts: There are two fabrics in each of these colors, so mix it up! Refer to the drawing for placement. Templates are on page 120. Onto the paper-backed adhesive, trace a large bunny and four small ones facing right and one large and four small ones facing left. Trace 11 hearts. Cut out the shapes leaving approximately ¼" of paper beyond the pencil line.

Yellows • (Cut one strip 2½" x 42" for Patch B before creating appliqué shapes.) Fuse two small bunnies, one large bunny, and two hearts to the back of the remaining fabric. Cut out the shapes on the pencil lines.
Lavenders • (Cut one strip 2½" x 42" for Patch B before creating appliqué shapes.) Fuse three small bunnies, one large bunny, and three hearts to the back of the remaining fabric. Cut out the shapes on the pencil lines.
Pinks • Fuse three hearts to the back of the fabric and cut out on the pencil lines.
Peaches • (Cut peach borders before creating appliqué shapes.) Fuse three small bunnies and three hearts to the back of the remaining fabric. Cut out the shapes on the pencil lines.
Pinwheels • These are made up of the scraps from the other quilt pieces. Cut a total of 56 squares 2⅞" x 2⅞". Cut in half diagonally for Patch D.

Peach Print for Border and Piecing
½ yard

Patch F: Cut three strips 2" x 42" strips. Join into one long strip. From this strip cut two strips 24½" for the sides; cut two strips 27½" for the top and bottom.

Continued on next page.

SUPPLIES

Backing
1½ yards

Batting 39" x 53"

Sewable Fusible
Paper-Backed Adhesive
1¼ yards

Stabilizer for
Machine Appliqué
1 yard

CUTTING

Backing: Cut one piece 39" x 53".

SEWING INSTRUCTIONS FOR BUNNY MELODY

*Review the Quilting Basics in
Chapter 2 before you begin.*

1. Make 14 Pinwheel blocks
following the instructions on
page 57.

2. Stitch white A1 to light green
A2. Press the seam allowances
toward the darker color.

3. Fuse the bunnies and hearts
to A1 and A2. Refer to the quilt
drawing for placement.

4. Sew the two fabric strips
for Patch B together to make
the alternating square border,
referring to page 103. Sew three
units (six squares) together for
each side border and remove
the yellow square from one
end. Sew six units (12 squares)
together for top and bottom
borders, and remove the lavender
square from one end.

5. Attach the alternating square
border to the quilt, following the
border instructions on page 33.

6. Add medium green (C) side
border pieces to the quilt, then
to the top and bottom.

7. Assemble three Pinwheel
blocks and three Heart blocks in
a row for the top, and then for
the bottom of the quilt. Sew to
the quilt.

8. Add second peach (F) side
border pieces to the quilt, then
to the top and bottom.

9. Fuse Bunnies and Hearts to
white (G) panels, referring to the
photo on page 104.

10. Add the Bunny panels (G) to
the top and bottom of the quilt.

11. Assemble the side borders
(two medium green I's and a
Pinwheel block) and sew to the
quilt. Assemble the top and
bottom borders (two medium
green H's and three Pinwheels),
and sew them to the quilt.

12. Follow the instructions on
page 35 for basting the quilt.

13. This quilt is hand-quilted
along all of the major seam lines.
Behind the appliqués, the
background is quilted diagonally
with lines 1" apart. Find a quilting
design you like to use in the
border areas.

14. Following the instructions on
page 37 for binding the quilt.

Bunny Melody Quilt Drawing

BUNNY HOP

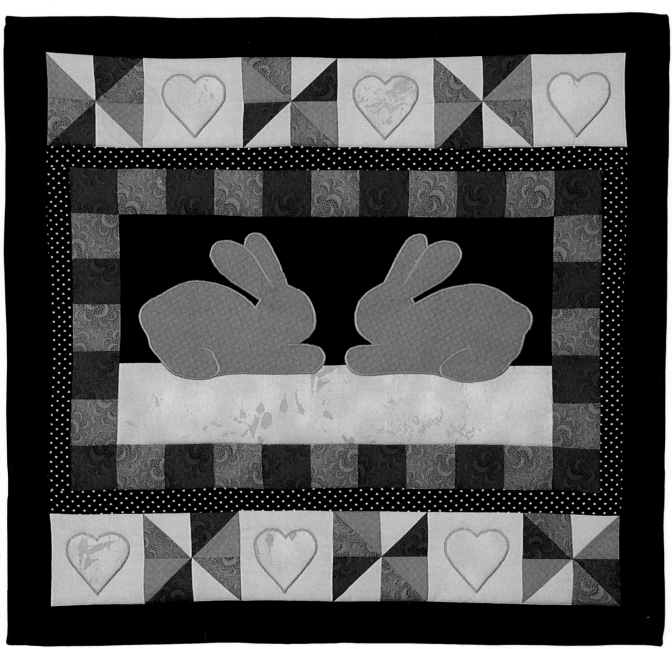

The finished size is 27½" x 27½".

Refer to quilt drawing and photo for color placement.

SUPPLIES	CUTTING

Black Solid for Background, F Border, and Binding
¾ yard

A1 Background: Cut one strip 7" x 18½".
F Border: Cut three strips 2" x 42". Join into one long strip. From this strip cut two strips 24½" for the sides; cut two strips 27½" for the top and bottom.
Binding: Cut three strips 1¾" x 42". Join in one long strip. From this strip cut two strips 27½" for the sides; cut two strips 28" for the top and bottom.

Black and White Polka Dot for C Border
⅛ yard

C Border: Cut two strips 1½" x 42". Open the strips and stack them. Cut two strips 14½" for the sides; cut two strips 24½" for the top and bottom.

Light Green Print for Grass and Hearts
⅛ yard

A2 Background: Cut one strip 4" x 18½".
Hearts: (Template is on page 120.) Trace six hearts onto the paper-backed adhesive. Trim around each, leaving ¼" of paper beyond the pencil line. Fuse the hearts to the wrong side of the light green fabric. Cut out the shapes on the pencil line.

Purple
¼ yard

Light Purple
¼ yard

Lavender
¼ yard

Green
⅛ yard

Green • Cut one strip 2½" x 42" for Patch B. Then cut one strip 4½" x 28" and cut into six squares 4½" x 4½" for Patch E.
Purple • Cut one strip 1½" x 42" for Patch B.
Light Purple • Template is on page 121. Trace two large bunnies facing each other onto the paper-backed adhesive. Trim around each, leaving ¼" of paper beyond the pencil line. Fuse the bunnies to the wrong side of the light purple fabric. Cut out the shapes on the pencil lines.
All four fabrics • Cut 24 squares 2⅞" x 2⅞"; cut in half diagonally for Pinwheels.

Backing
1 yard

Backing: Cut one piece 32" x 32".

Batting 32" x 32"

Sewable Fusible Paper-backed Adhesive
½ yard

Stabilizer for Machine Appliqué
½ yard

Sewing instructions begin on next page.

SEWING INSTRUCTIONS FOR BUNNY HOP

Review the Quilting Basics in Chapter 2 before you begin.

1. Make six Pinwheel blocks following the instructions on page 57.

2. Stitch black A1 to light green A2 to create the background for the bunnies. Press toward black A1.

3. Appliqué the Bunnies to their background following the instructions on pages 31-32. Appliqué the Hearts to the pink squares. Refer to quilt drawing for placement.

4. Sew the two strips for Patch B together to make the alternating square border, referring to page 103. Sew three units (six squares) together for each side border and remove the yellow square from one end. Sew six units (12 squares) together for top and bottom borders, and remove the lavender square from one end. Sew the alternating square border to the quilt.

Bunny Hop Quilt Drawing

5. Add black print (C) borders to the quilt following directions on page 33.

6. Join Pinwheels and Hearts made earlier for the top and bottom borders of the quilt. Add to the quilt.

7. Add black (F) borders to the quilt following directions on page 33.

8. Follow the instructions on page 35 for basting the quilt.

9. This quilt was machine-quilted along the seam lines and around the appliqué shapes. Refer to the photo for quilting ideas.

10. Follow the instructions on page 37 for binding the quilt.

CHECKERBOARD BUNNIES

The finished size is 38½" x 54½".

Refer to quilt drawing and photo for color placement.

SUPPLIES	CUTTING

Background Panels and Binding
1⅓ yards

Background Panels: For two A panels, cut two strips 8½" x 30½". For two B panels, cut two strips 4½" x 30½". For one C panel, cut one strip 10½" x 30½".
Binding: Cut five strips 1¾" x 42". Join into one long strip. From this strip cut two strips 54½" for the sides; cut two strips 39" for the top and bottom.

Checkerboard and Large Bunnies
½ yard

Second Color for Checkerboard
⅓ yard

Yellow for Stars
¼ yard

Gold for Moon
¼ yard

Pink and Green for Hearts
⅛ yard each of two colors

Checkerboard: Cut four 2" x 42" strips of each color.
Appliqués: Templates are on pages 120-121. For machine appliqué, trace three large bunnies facing left, six stars, two moons, and six hearts on the paper-backed adhesive. Cut around the shapes ¼" beyond the pencil lines. Fuse to the wrong side of their respective fabric colors. Cut out the shapes on the pencil line.

Border
⅔ yard

Borders: Cut five strips 4½" x 42". Join into one long strip. From this strip cut two strips 46½" for the sides; cut two strips 38½" for the top and bottom.

Backing
1⅔ yards

Backing: Cut one piece 43" x 59".

Batting 43" x 59"

Sewable Fusible Paper-backed Adhesive
1¼ yards

Stabilizer for Machine Appliqué
1¼ yards

SEWING INSTRUCTIONS FOR CHECKERBOARD BUNNIES

Review the Quilting Basics in Chapter 2 before you begin.

1. To make the checkerboard, sew a strip of each color together and press toward the darker fabric. Repeat with the second set of strips. Cut across the strips at 2" intervals, referring to page 103.

2. Stitch 20 pairs together in alternating colors to create a checkerboard. Repeat to make four checkerboard strips.

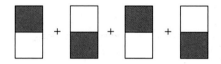

3. Join the panels to the checker-boards as shown in the drawing.

4. Follow the instructions on page 33 to complete the outside border.

5. *(The following instructions are for machine appliqué. If you wish to hand appliqué, refer to the instructions on page 31.)* Fuse the bunnies, stars, moons, and hearts to the wrong side of their respective colors. Cut out the shapes on the pencil line and fuse to the quilt top, following manufacturer's instructions. Refer to the quilt drawing for placement.

6. Machine appliqué the shapes following the instructions on page 31.

7. Follow the instructions on page 35 for basting the quilt.

Checkerboard Bunnies Quilt Drawing

8. This quilt was machine-quilted along the seam lines and around the appliqué shapes.

9. Follow the instructions on page 37 for binding the quilt.

RABBIT PATCH

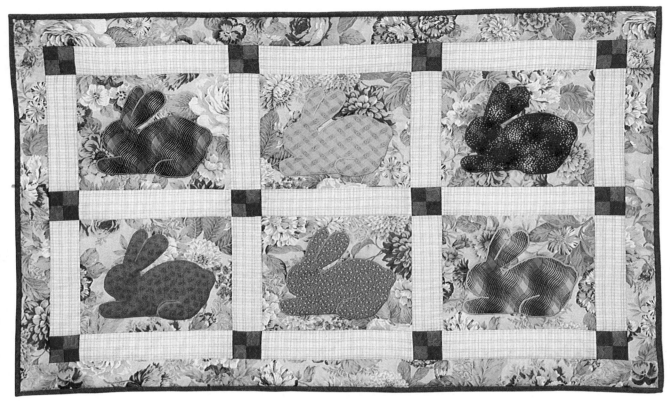

The finished size is 26½" x 42½". The block size is 8" x 10".

Refer to quilt drawing and photo for color placement.

SUPPLIES

Floral Fabric for Background and Border
⅞ yard

Sashing
½ yard

Red Print for Four Patches and Binding
⅓ yard

Green Print for Four Patches
⅛ yard

Bunnies
7" x 9" each of six fabrics

Backing
1⅓ yards

Batting 31" x 47"

Stabilizer for Machine Appliqué
⅔ yard

Sewable Fusible Paper-backed Adhesive
⅔ yard

CUTTING

Background Blocks: Cut two strips 8½" x 42".
Cut into six rectangles 8½" x 10½"
Borders: Cut four strips 2½" x 42". Join into one long strip.
From this strip cut two strips 22½" for the sides; cut two strips 42½" for the top and bottom.

Sashes: Cut five strips 2½" x 42". Open the strips and stack two strips to cut eight strips 2½" x 8½". Stack the remaining three strips and cut nine strips 2½" x 10½".

Four Patches: Cut one strip 1½" x 42" of each color.
Binding: Cut four red strips 1¾" x 42". Join into one long strip.
From this strip cut two strips 26½" for the sides; cut two strips 43" for the top and bottom.

Appliqués: Template is on page 121. Trace six large bunnies facing right on the paper-backed adhesive. Trim around the rabbits ¼" beyond the pencil lines. Fuse one to the wrong side of each of the six bunny fabrics. Cut out the shapes on the pencil line.

Backing: Cut one piece 31" x 47".

Sewing instructions begin on next page.

SEWING INSTRUCTIONS FOR RABBIT PATCH

Rabbit Patch Quilt Drawing

Review the Quilting Basics in Chapter 2 before you begin.

1. To make the Four-Patch corners, sew the red and green 1½" strips together. Press toward darker color. Cut across at 1½" intervals, referring to page 103. Sew two pairs together to create a Four Patch. Make 12 Four Patches.

2. Fuse the bunnies to the floral blocks.

3. Machine appliqué the bunnies following the instructions on page 31.

4. Lay out the quilt blocks, inserting the sashing and Four Patch corners. Refer to photograph for placement of Bunny blocks. Sew together in rows. Row 1 will be sashing and Four-Patches. Row 2 will be sashing and blocks. Follow the straight set instructions on page 33 for sewing the blocks together.

5. Follow the instructions on page 33 for adding the border.

6. Follow the instructions on pages 35 for basting the quilt.

7. This quilt was machine-quilted along the seam lines and around the appliqué shapes.

8. Follow the instructions on page 37 for binding the quilt.

GARDEN VARIETY

The finished size is 37" x 37". The block size is 6" x 8".

Refer to quilt drawing and photo for color placement.

SUPPLIES

CUTTING

Background Blocks
⅝ yard or 7" x 9" scraps of 12 fabrics

Background Blocks: Cut 12 rectangles 6½" x 8½".
Bunnies: Template is on page 120. Trace seven small bunnies facing right and five small bunnies facing left on the paper-backed adhesive. Trim around the bunnies ¼" beyond the pencil line. Fuse to wrong side of the bunny fabric. Cut out the bunnies on the pencil line.

Bunnies
⅜ yard or 5" x 7" scraps of 12 Black Print fabrics

Dark Color for Checkerboard
¼ yard

Checkerboard: Cut four strips 1½" x 42" each of dark and light fabrics.

Light Color for Checkerboard
¼ yard

Three Darks and Three Lights for Pinwheels
⅛ yard each

Pinwheel Blocks: Cut a strip 2⅜" x 42" from all six fabrics. Open the strips and stack them with right sides of a matching dark and light fabric together. Cut strips into 12 squares 2⅜" x 2⅜". Cut in half diagonally. (This yields six Pinwheels of each color combination. You need a total of 16 Pinwheels.)

First Border
⅛ yard

First Border: Cut four strips 1" x 32¼".
Use the templates on page 34 to cut 45° angle for mitered borders.

Second Border
½ yard

Second Border: Cut four strips 3¼" x 37¼".
Use the templates on page 34 to cut 45° angle for mitered borders.

Binding
¼ yard

Binding: Cut four strips 1¾" x 42". Open the strips. Cut two strips 37" for the sides; cut two strips 37½" for the top and bottom.

Backing
1¼ yards

Backing: Cut one piece 41" x 41".

Batting 41" x 41"

Sewable Fusible Paper-backed Adhesive
⅔ yard

Stabilizer for Machine Appliqué
⅔ yard

SEWING INSTRUCTIONS FOR GARDEN VARIETY

Review the Quilting Basics in Chapter 2 before you begin.

1. Appliqué the bunnies to the background block. See page 32. Make 12 Bunny blocks.

2. Make 16 Pinwheel blocks. Refer to instructions on page 57.

3. Construct three strips of checkerboard squares that are 30½" long (30 squares in each strip). Refer to page 103.

4. Refer to the drawing and construct each horizontal row of the quilt. Follow the straight set instructions on page 33 for sewing the blocks together.

5. Follow the instructions on page 34 for adding the mitered borders.

6. Follow the instructions on page 35 for basting the quilt.

7. This quilt is hand-quilted but could be easily machine-quilted. The bunnies are outlined, and the blocks are stitched in-the-ditch.

8. Follow the instructions on page 37 for binding the quilt.

Garden Variety Quilt Drawing

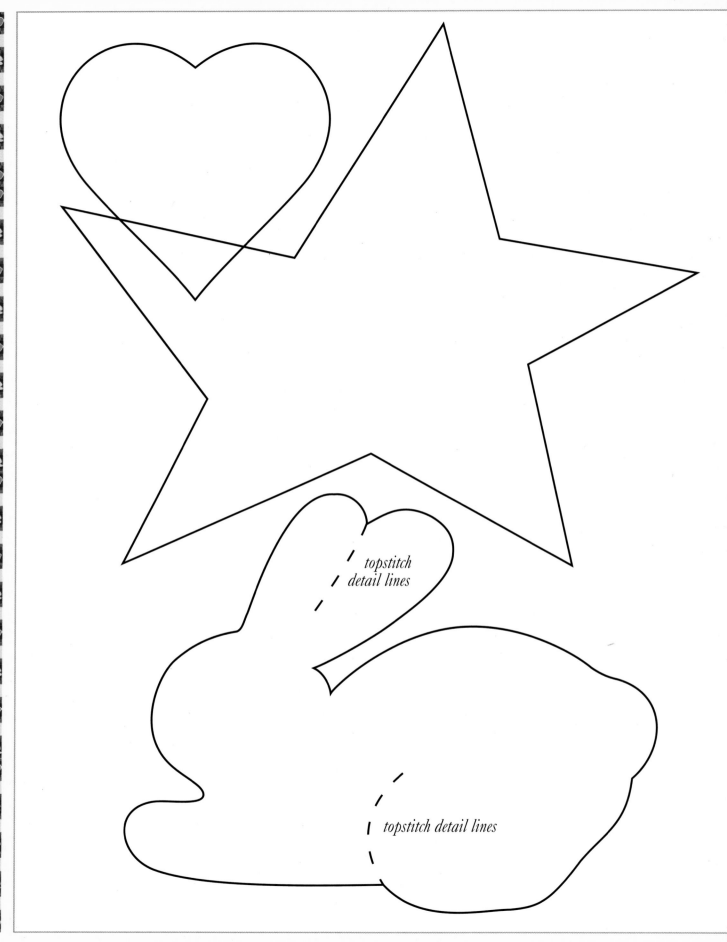

topstitch
detail lines

topstitch detail lines

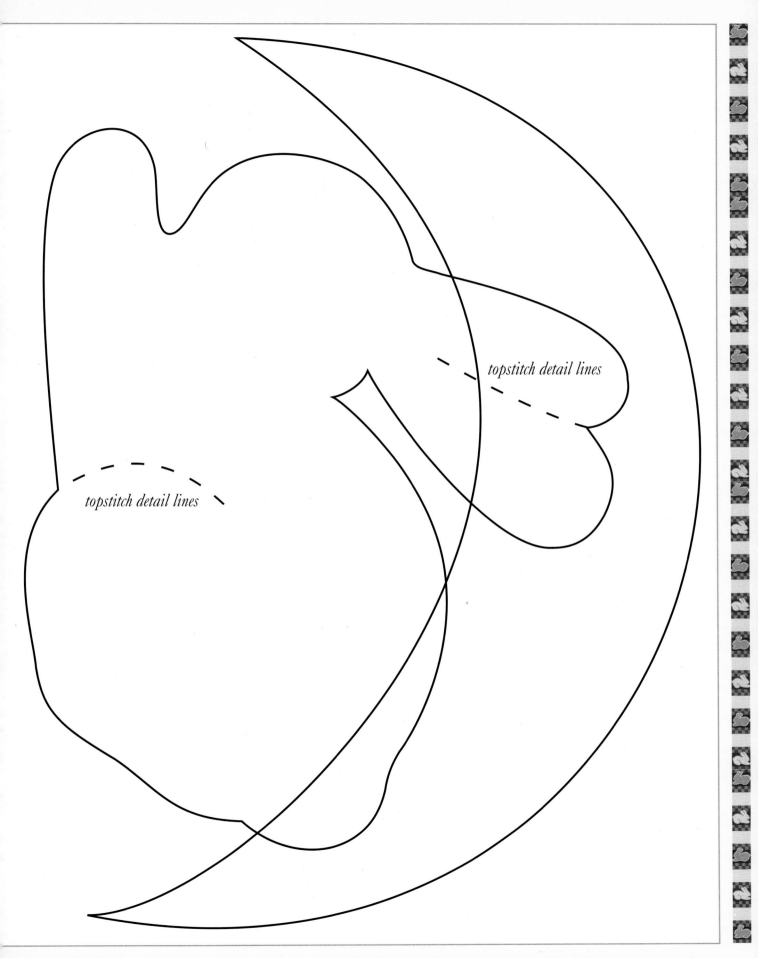

topstitch detail lines

topstitch detail lines

121

STARS AND HEARTS QUILTS

CHAPTER EIGHT

Stars and Hearts Quilts

The *Stars and Hearts* quilt design was generated out of my doodlings. Although I'm sure I'm not the first person that ever came up with the design, I was playing with the idea of simple block designs combined with an appliqué block. *Stars and Hearts* was born. As you can see from these quilts, the design lends itself to soft pastels, to a dramatic two-color quilt, and to a traditional quilt.

In *Star Formation* the print fabric is used in the centers of the stars as well as on the star points, thus filling the whole stars. The elongated-looking star shapes on a smaller scale would be a great repeat in a border. When choosing the fabrics for this quilt, I was able to find a border stripe that matched the star. Stripes create a flowing feeling when used lengthwise. If the stripes are to meet at the corners, then they should be mitered. (See page 34 for mitering instructions.) In the case of the quilt pictured, one of the pieced blocks was placed in each of the corners.

When I chose the theme fabric for *Hearts and Flowers*, I wanted one that would fit into a pastel, feminine setting. I can see this quilt draped over a wicker chair or in a white baby crib. Notice how different each heart design is. Cutting the heart shape from a large print creates a one-of-a-kind design.

Scrap Bag Stars is a variation on this theme. I had always wanted to try the pattern where the blocks weren't alternated. I picked three different lights, a variety of darks, and a couple of mediums. Then they were cut into quarter-square triangles and squares.

To create a random design like this, you need to work on a piece of flannel or dense batting that is pinned to a wall. The fabric will stick to the flannel as you place it. Start creating the patch units, inserting a heart block here and there. Every so often back up and look at the design from a distance. Make adjustments until you like what you see.

In this quilt there are two hidden stars. The red one is obvious, but the second one is more subtle. When I finished this quilt, I felt I had created something really special from a scrap bag.

STARS AND HEARTS BLOCK INSTRUCTIONS

A combination of easy appliqué and easy piecing will yield Stars and Hearts on your quiltmaking journey. Read through all of the general instructions before you begin these projects.

Pieced Block

The Stars and Hearts quilts are two-block quilts. The first block is pieced and the second one is a square with an appliquéd heart. In most of the quilts, a heart is appliquéd in the square; in *Star Formation*, there are no hearts. Refer to the drawings for each quilt to see how many blocks are in the rows and how many rows are in the quilt.

1. To construct the pieced block, place right sides together of the dark and medium triangles, with the medium triangle on top.

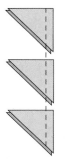 **2.** Line up the pairs of fabrics as shown. Stitch pairs together along one of the short sides. Whenever possible, feed pairs of fabric through the sewing machine, one after the other, without lifting the presser foot. There will be a chain of stitches between the units, creating a string of stitched units.

3. Remove the chain of sewn patches from the machine. Clip the threads between the pairs to release them. Press both seam allowances toward the darker fabric.

4. Pick up two of the pressed units. Place right sides together. The seam allowances will automatically go in opposite directions and nest together. Pin the units together if you feel it is necessary.

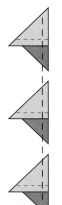 **5.** Stitch these together along the long side, using the chaining method, then clip them apart, and press in either direction.

6. Trim off the points of the seam allowances even with the blocks. Set the units aside.

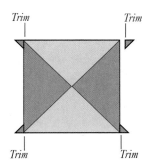

Heart Appliqué Block

Follow the instructions on page 32 to make the fusible appliqué blocks. Large and small heart templates are on page 135.

LOVING STARS

The finished size is 64½" x 88½". The block size is 4".

Refer to quilt drawing and photo for color placement.

SUPPLIES

CUTTING

Stars
1⅔ yards each of dark and medium fabric

Dark Quarter-Square Triangles (Patch A): Cut 11 strips 5¼" x 42". Open the strips and stack them in layers of four. Cut eight squares 5¼" x 5¼" from each layer of strips. Leave these in their stacks. (You will need 88 squares.) Cut the squares into quarters diagonally. (There will be 352 triangles.)
Medium Quarter-Square Triangles: Repeat the above cutting instructions for the medium color.

Heart Background Blocks
2⅝ yards of light fabric

Heart Background Blocks (Patch B): Cut 20 strips 4½" x 42". Open the strips and stack them in layers of four. Cut nine squares 4½" x 4½" from each stack of strips. (You will need 176.)

Hearts
2⅛ yards of red fabric

Hearts (Patch C): Trace 176 small hearts (template on page 135) on the paper-backed adhesive. Seven will fit in a row. Fuse the hearts to the wrong side of the fabric. Cut out the hearts on the pencil line.

Binding
½ yard of dark fabric

Binding: Cut eight strips 1¾" x 42". Join into one long strip. From this strip cut two strips 88½" for the sides; cut two strips 65" for the top and bottom.

Backing
5¼ yards

Backing: Cut two pieces of fabric 42" x 93". Trim off the selvages and sew sections together, right sides facing, along the lengthwise grain.

Batting 69" x 93"

Sewable Fusible
Paper-backed Adhesive
3¾ yards

SEWING INSTRUCTIONS FOR LOVING STARS

Review the Quilting Basics in Chapter 2 before you begin.

1. Follow the pieced block directions on page 125 and make 176 blocks.

2. Follow the fusible appliqué instructions on page 32 and make 176 Heart blocks.

3. Arrange the blocks in rows, alternating a pieced block with an appliqué block. There will be 16 blocks across, in 22 rows. Follow the straight set instructions on page 33 for sewing the blocks together.

4. Follow the instructions on page 35 for basting the quilt.

5. Machine-quilt in-the-ditch.

6. Follow the instructions on page 37 for binding the quilt.

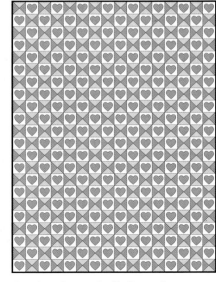

Loving Stars Quilt Drawing

STAR FORMATION

The finished size is 25½" x 33½". The block size is 4".

Refer to quilt drawing and photo for color placement.

SUPPLIES

Print forStars and Light Corners
⅓ yard

Print for Background and Dark Corners
⅜ yard

First Border
⅛ yard

Second Border
⅝ yard (¾ yard for striped fabric, cut lengthwise)

Binding
¼ yard

Backing
⅞ yard

Batting 30" x 38"

CUTTING

Stars and Light Corners: Cut one strip 5¼" x 42". Cut into nine squares 5¼" x 5¼". Cut one additional 5¼" square. You will have 10 squares. Cut the squares into quarters diagonally (there will be 40). Cut one strip 4½" x 19". Cut into four squares 4½" x 4½".

Background and Dark Corners: Cut one strip 5¼" x 42". Cut five squares 5¼" x 5¼". Cut the squares into quarters diagonally. (There will be 20.) Using the leftover strip, cut four squares 2⅞" x 2⅞". Cut them in half diagonally. Cut one strip 4½" x 42". Cut four squares 4½" x 4½" and eight rectangles 4½" x 2½".

First Border: Cut two strips 1" x 42". Open the strips and stack them. Cut two strips 24½" for the sides; cut two strips 17½" for the top and bottom.

Second Border: If you have chosen a striped fabric, cut the four strips on the lengthwise grain. Otherwise, cut three strips 4½" x 42". Join into one long strip. From this strip cut two strips 25½" for the two sides; cut two strips 17½" for top and bottom.

Binding: Cut three strips 1¾" x 42". Join into one long strip. From this strip cut two strips 33½" for the sides; cut two strips 26" for the top and bottom.

Backing: Cut one piece 30" x 38".

Sewing instructions begin on next page.

SEWING INSTRUCTIONS FOR STAR FORMATION

Review the Quilting Basics in Chapter 2 before you begin.

1. Follow the pieced block directions on page 125 and make six blocks: two are used in quilt center; four are used in border corners.

2. Make eight blocks with three of the triangles in star fabric and one in background fabric (see quilt drawing). Place the right side of the background fabric triangle on the right side of the star fabric triangle along the short edge. Stitch. Make eight units, following Steps 1 to 3 on page 125. Press toward the dark fabric.

3. Place two star fabric triangles right sides together. Stitch eight units along the short edge. Press. The remainder of the block is stitched exactly like the basic block.

4. In this quilt there is a half block at the side. To construct the side block star point, place the long side of the small half-square triangle (dark fabric) on the short side of the larger half-square triangle (light fabric). Stitch the seam. Press toward the small triangle. Trim off the seam allowance points even with the block. Stitch four units.

Stitch and flip.

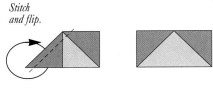

5. Repeat on the other side of the block. Stitch four units. Press.

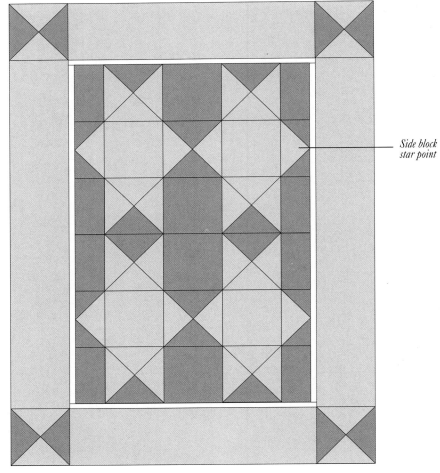

Star Formation Quilt Drawing

Side block star point

6. The rows are constructed as shown in the figure below. Place the blocks in rows on your work surface. Follow the straight set instructions on page 33 for sewing the blocks together.

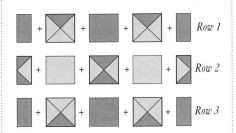

7. Follow the instructions on page 33 for adding borders.

8. Follow the instructions on page 35 for basting the layers.

9. This quilt is machine-quilted in-the-ditch along the Star seam lines.

10. Follow the instructions on page 37 for binding the wall hanging.

SCRAP BAG STARS

The finished size is 28½" x 32½". The block size is 4".

Refer to quilt drawing and photo for color placement.

SUPPLIES

 Medium Dark and Dark Prints scraps to total 1 yard

Medium Light and Light Prints scraps to total 1 yard

 Binding ¼ yard

Backing ⅞ yard

Batting 33" x 37"

Plastic-coated Freezer Paper ⅝ yard

CUTTING

Pieced Blocks: For the pieced unit you will need a total of 76 dark and 76 light quarter-square triangles. Since you are using scraps, cut 19 light and 19 dark squares 5¼" x 5¼" each for a total of 38 squares. Cut into quarters diagonally.

Heart Background Blocks: Cut 18 squares 4½" x 4½" from medium light and light prints.

Hearts: Cut 18 squares 4" x 4" from medium dark and dark prints. Do not cut out the small hearts (template on page 135) until you determine the appliqué method that you will use. Refer to pages 31-32 for ideas. I hand-appliquéd the hearts on my quilt.

Binding: Cut four strips 1¾" x 42". From these strips cut two strips 28½" for the sides; cut two strips 33" for the top and bottom.

Backing: Cut one piece 33" x 37"

SEWING INSTRUCTIONS FOR SCRAP BAG STARS

Review the Quilting Basics in Chapter 2 before you begin.

1. Follow the pieced block instructions on page 125 to make 38 pieced blocks.

2. Determine the method of appliqué you will use on the 18 Heart blocks and appliqué the hearts onto the heart background blocks (see pages 31-32).

3. Arrange the blocks in rows. Follow the straight set instructions on page 33 for sewing the blocks together.

4. Follow the instructions on page 35 for basting the quilt.

5. This quilt is machine-quilted in-the-ditch and hand-quilted around the stars.

6. Follow the instructions on page 37 for binding the quilt.

Scrap Bag Stars Quilt Drawing

HEARTS AND FLOWERS

The finished size is 37½" x 47½". The block size is 5".

Refer to quilt drawing and photo for color placement.

SUPPLIES

CUTTING

Print Stars, Second Border, and Hearts
1½ yards

Print Stars: Cut two strips 6¼" x 42" of print star fabric. Open the strips and stack them. Cut 11 squares 6¼" x 6¼". Cut the squares into quarters diagonally. (There will be 44.)
First Border Corner Stars: Cut two squares 1⅞" x 1⅞" of print fabric. Cut in half diagonally.
Second Border: Cut four strips 5½" x 42". From these strips cut two strips 37½" for the sides; cut two strips 27½" for the top and bottom.
Hearts: Trace 17 large hearts (template on page 135) on the paper-backed adhesive. Fuse to the wrong side of the fabric. Cut out the hearts on the pencil line.

Solid Stars
⅜ yard

Solid Stars: Repeat the cutting instructions above for Print Stars.
First Border Corner Stars: Cut two squares 1⅞" x 1⅞" of solid fabric. Cut in half diagonally.

Heart Background Blocks
½ yard

Heart Background Blocks: Cut three strips 5½" x 42" each. Open the strips and stack them. Cut 17 squares 5½" x 5½".

First Border
¼ yard

First Border: Cut three strips 1½" x 42". Join into one long strip. From this strip cut two strips 35½" for the sides; cut two strips 25½" for the top and bottom.

Binding
¼ yard

Binding: Cut four strips 1¾" x 42". Join into one long strip. From this strip cut two strips 47½" for the sides; cut two strips 38" for the top and bottom.

Backing
1½ yards

Backing: Cut one piece 42" x 52".

Batting 42" x 52"

Sewable Fusible Paper-Backed Adhesive
⅞ yard

SEWING INSTRUCTIONS FOR HEARTS AND FLOWERS

Review the Quilting Basics in Chapter 2 before you begin.

1. Follow the pieced block directions on page 125 and make 22 pieced blocks (see quilt drawing).

2. Follow the fusible appliqué instructions on page 32 and make 18 Heart blocks.

3. Arrange the blocks in rows, alternating a pieced block with an appliqué block. There will be five blocks across, in seven rows. Follow the straight set instructions on page 33 for sewing the blocks together.

4. Stitch the small half-square triangles of the print fabric to the small half-square triangles of the solid fabric along the long side. Make four units for the corners of the first border.

5. Follow the instructions on page 33 for adding the borders.

6. Follow the instructions on page 35 for basting the quilt layers.

7. This quilt was machine-quilted along the seam lines.

8. Follow the instructions on page 37 for binding the quilt.

Hearts and Flowers Quilt Drawing

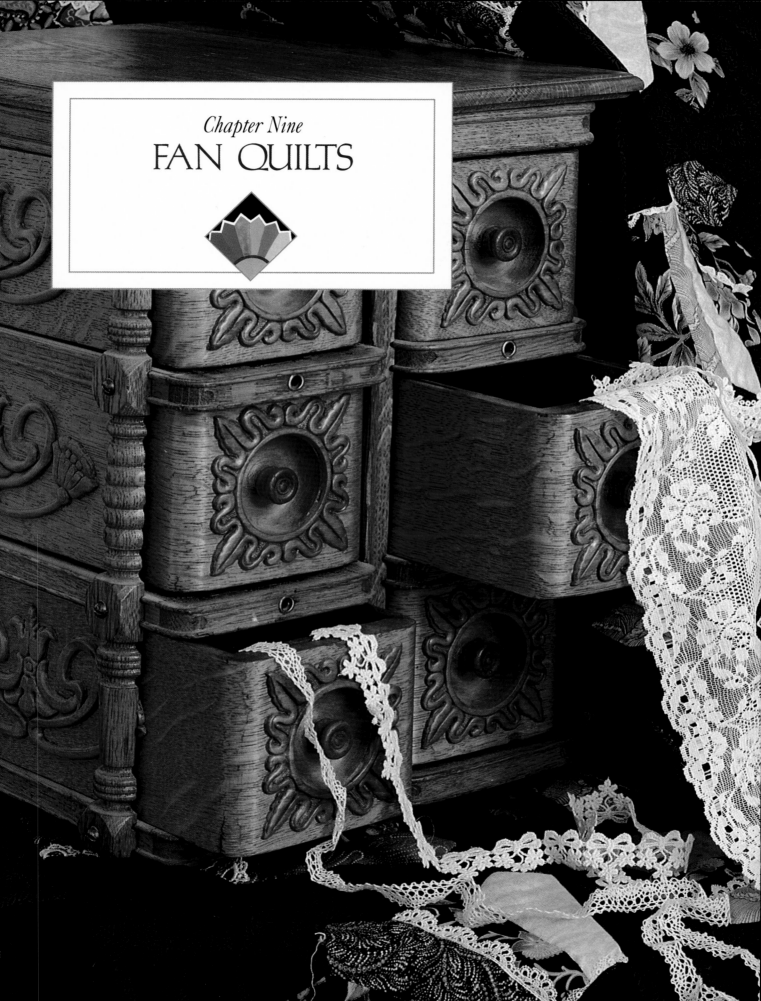

Chapter Nine
FAN QUILTS

CHAPTER NINE

Fan Quilts

Twelve years ago, I wrote a book on making Fan quilts so they have always had a special place in my heart. The fan shape set into a corner of a background block is often on its side. If you place it on point, the fan is straight as you view it. The quilts in this chapter show fans in many settings. As you view the quilts, you will see fans with pointed wedges and rounded wedges. The bottom of the fan is called the base. Fabrics for the wedges can be all from the same print or different ones, depending on the look that you want. The fan pieces can be appliquéd to the background block or pieced to a background shape.

Bow Tie Fans is a setting that I saw on an antique family quilt owned by Dorothy Taylor, a fellow quiltmaker. Notice how the fans come together at the base and form a modified bow tie. By using a dark base and medium-dark background fabric, the bases almost disappear when seen from a distance. Very narrow flat lace decorates each base and the edges between some of the blades.

For my birthday this year, Liz Aneloski, my editor, surprised me with *Lacy Fans*. If you look closely, you'll see there are no pieced fans on this quilt. The fan shapes are made by cutting lace doilies in quarters and appliquéing them to a square. This is an easy way to create a "fancy" design. Liz's color choices came from the small floral print border. I added the button clusters and narrow rickrack trim to the edges.

In the black, white, pink and green quilt, all of the colors are high contrast. When it was finished, it reminded me of *Watermelon Slices* so that is how it got its title. On page 21, the photo shows the little ceramic chair that inspired the palette for this quilt. The chair and the quilt remind me of Mary Engelbreit's paintings. I love her work. She uses a lot of black and white with bright colors, so she was an inspiration in my choice of fabrics. This 6" block is so simple that you will enjoy the easy curved piecing. Notice the borders in many widths. This is an effective way to tie in fabrics from the center with the borders.

Creams and whites are among my favorite palettes. When you work with colors like these, there will not be as much contrast, but the subtlety creates a mellow, elegant mood that has a Victorian feeling. *Crazy Patch* uses a pieced crazy-patch technique for the fan shape. Stitch the pieces in the numbered order for easy construction.

FAN BLOCK INSTRUCTIONS

Fan quilts add a gentle curve to your piecing skills. Laces and buttons can be added for an elegant appearance. Read through all of the general instructions before you begin these projects.

Fan Block Construction

There are two different methods of Fan block construction that will be explained here. Templates will be made for the various pieces (see pages 142, 145-146, 152-153).

Pointed-Wedge Fan

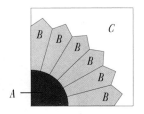

1. Cut six B's using the template on page 142. Also cut one A, using the template, and one C.

2. Fold the wedge wrong sides together lengthwise. Stitch across the top. Trim where indicated.

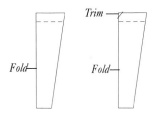

3. Turn to the right side and press. Make sure the seam allowance is open. You will have perfect points the easy way!

Press seam open.

4. Stitch the six wedges together, sewing from the top of the wedge to the bottom. Flat lace may be inserted between the wedges if desired.

5. Place flat lace facing away from the curved edge of A so the edge of the lace is ¼" from the cut edge. Stitch.

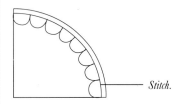

Stitch.

6. Turn to the right side. Sometimes it may be necessary to snip between the repeats on the lace. Press.

7. Place A on B. Topstitch by machine or appliqué by hand in place. Repeat by placing B on C and topstitching or appliquéing in place.

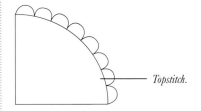

Topstitch.

6" Fan

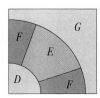

1. Using templates on pages 152-153, cut out one D, E, G, and two F's.

2. Stitch F to each side of E. Press seam allowances toward E.

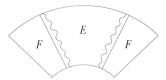

3. To add D to FEF, finely clip the curve on FEF every ¼" in about ⅛" increments.

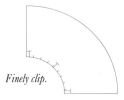

Finely clip.

4. Mark the center of D and FEF with a pin. Place right sides together, matching pins. Line up the straight edges on the sides and pin at each end. With FEF facing you, stitch ¼" from the raw edges. Take it slowly, stitching about an inch and stopping. Reposition the fabric in front of you so the raw edges are together, then continue. (If you take it slowly and are careful, it will turn out perfectly!)

5. Clip G as you did FEF above and join to FEF.

BOW TIE FANS

The finished size is 74½" x 93½". The block size is 9½".

Refer to quilt drawing and photo for color placement.
Make a template for base A and fan wedge B (page 142).

SUPPLIES

Black for Base A, Second Border, and Binding
2½ yards

Variety of Prints for Fan Wedge B
5 yards total

Background C
4⅝ yards

First Border
⅜ yard

Backing
5½ yards

Batting 79" x 98"

¼" flat lace for Base A
11 yards

Optional: Additional lace between wedges

CUTTING

Base A: Cut seven strips 4" x 42". Open the strips and stack them in groups of three. Use Base A template to cut 63.

Second Border: Cut eight strips 3¼" x 42". Join in one long strip. From this strip cut two strips 88" for the sides; cut two strips 74½" for the top and bottom.

Binding: Cut nine strips 1¾" x 42". Join in one long strip. From this strip cut two strips 93½" for the sides; cut two strips 75" for the top and bottom.

Fan Wedge B: Cut 27 strips 6½" x 42". Open the strips and stack them in groups of three. Use fan wedge template on page 142 to cut out 378 wedges.

Background C: Cut 16 strips 10" x 42". Cut 63 squares 10" x 10".

First Border: Cut eight strips 1½" x 42". Join into one long strip. From this strip cut two strips 86" for the sides; cut two strips 69" for the top and bottom.

Backing: Cut two pieces 42" x 98". Trim off the selvages and sew sections together, right sides facing, along the lengthwise grain.

SEWING INSTRUCTIONS FOR BOW TIE FANS

Review the Quilting Basics in Chapter 2 before you begin.

1. Construct 63 Fans following the Pointed-wedge Fan directions on page 139. Attach to background blocks.

2. Follow the quilt drawing and arrange the blocks in rows. Follow the straight set instructions on page 33 for sewing the blocks together.

3. Follow the instructions on page 33 for adding the borders.

4. Follow the instructions on page 35 for basting the quilt.

5. This quilt was machine-quilted between the blocks, between the fan wedges, and around the base. Two rows of echo quilting were added in C.

6. Follow the instructions on page 37 for binding the quilt.

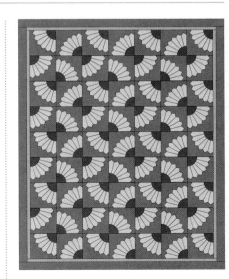

Bow Tie Fans Quilt Drawing

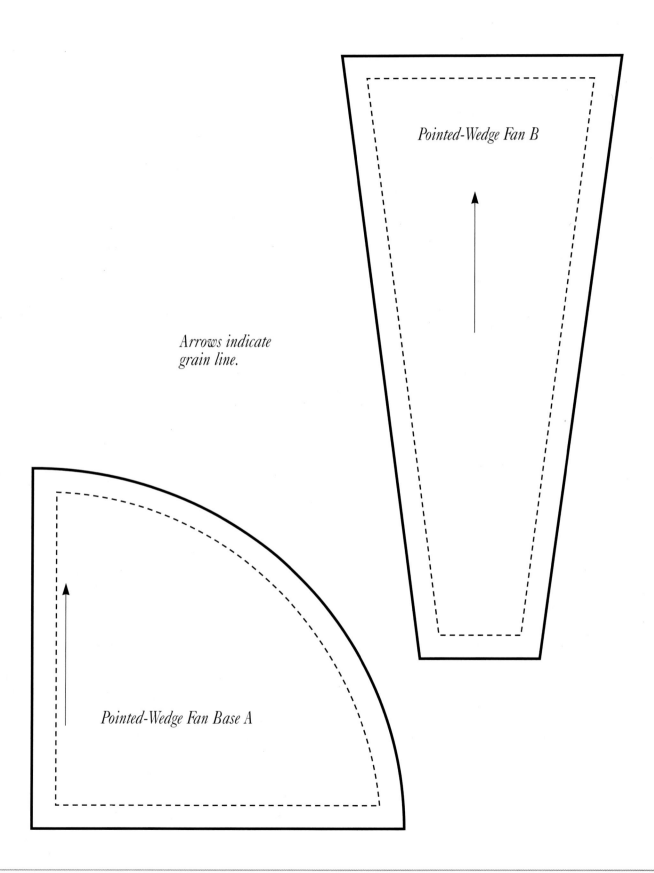

Pointed-Wedge Fan B

Arrows indicate
grain line.

Pointed-Wedge Fan Base A

CRAZY PATCH

The finished size is 21½" x 21½". The block size is 6".

Refer to quilt drawing and photo for color placement.

SUPPLIES

☐	**Crazy Patch Fan** ⅛ yard each of six fabrics
☐	**Base K, Background G,** **and Corner Squares** **for Border** ¼ yard
☐	**Accent Strip** ⅛ yard
☐	**Corner Triangles** ⅓ yard
☐	**Border** **and Binding** ⅜ yard
	Backing ¾ yard
	Batting 26" x 26"

CUTTING

Crazy Patch Fan: Using templates 1 through 6 on page 145 and a variety of fabrics, cut four fabric patches from each of the templates.

Base K: Cut four using template K on page 145.
Background G: Cut four using template G on page 146.
Corner Squares for Border: Cut four squares 2½" x 2½".

Accent Strip: Cut two strips 1" x 42". Open the strips and stack them. From these strips cut four strips 12½".

Corner Triangles: Cut two squares 9⅜" x 9⅜". Cut them in half diagonally.

Border: Cut two strips 2½" x 42". Open the strips and stack them. From these strips cut four strips 17½".
Binding: Cut three strips 1¾" x 42". Join into one long strip. From this strip cut two strips 21½" for the sides; cut two strips 22" for the top and bottom.

Backing: Cut one piece 26" x 26".

SEWING INSTRUCTIONS FOR CRAZY PATCH

Review the Quilting Basics in Chapter 2 before you begin.

1. To make the Crazy Patch Fan, stitch 1 and 2 together. Then stitch 3 and 4. Add to 1-2. Set aside. Stitch 5 to 3-4. Add 6. (*Optional:* Lace can be added in any of the seams as you stitch one seam to the next.)

2. Add base K and background G according to the 6" Fan instructions on page 139.

3. Follow the quilt drawing and the straight set instructions on page 33 to assemble the four Fan blocks.

4. Fold the accent strips in half lengthwise and press. Lay along each edge of the quilt and pin in place. See box on page 69.

5. Lay corner triangles over the folded accent strip on each side. Stitch through the blocks, accent strips, and corner triangles.

6. Follow the instructions on page 33 for adding the border.

7. Follow the instructions on page 35 for basting the quilt.

8. This quilt was hand-quilted. Quilting designs are included on page 146 for the fans, bases, and backgrounds. The border is quilted in 1"-wide diagonals. Use your cutting ruler to mark these.

Crazy Patch Quilt Drawing

9. Follow the instructions on page 37 for binding the quilt.

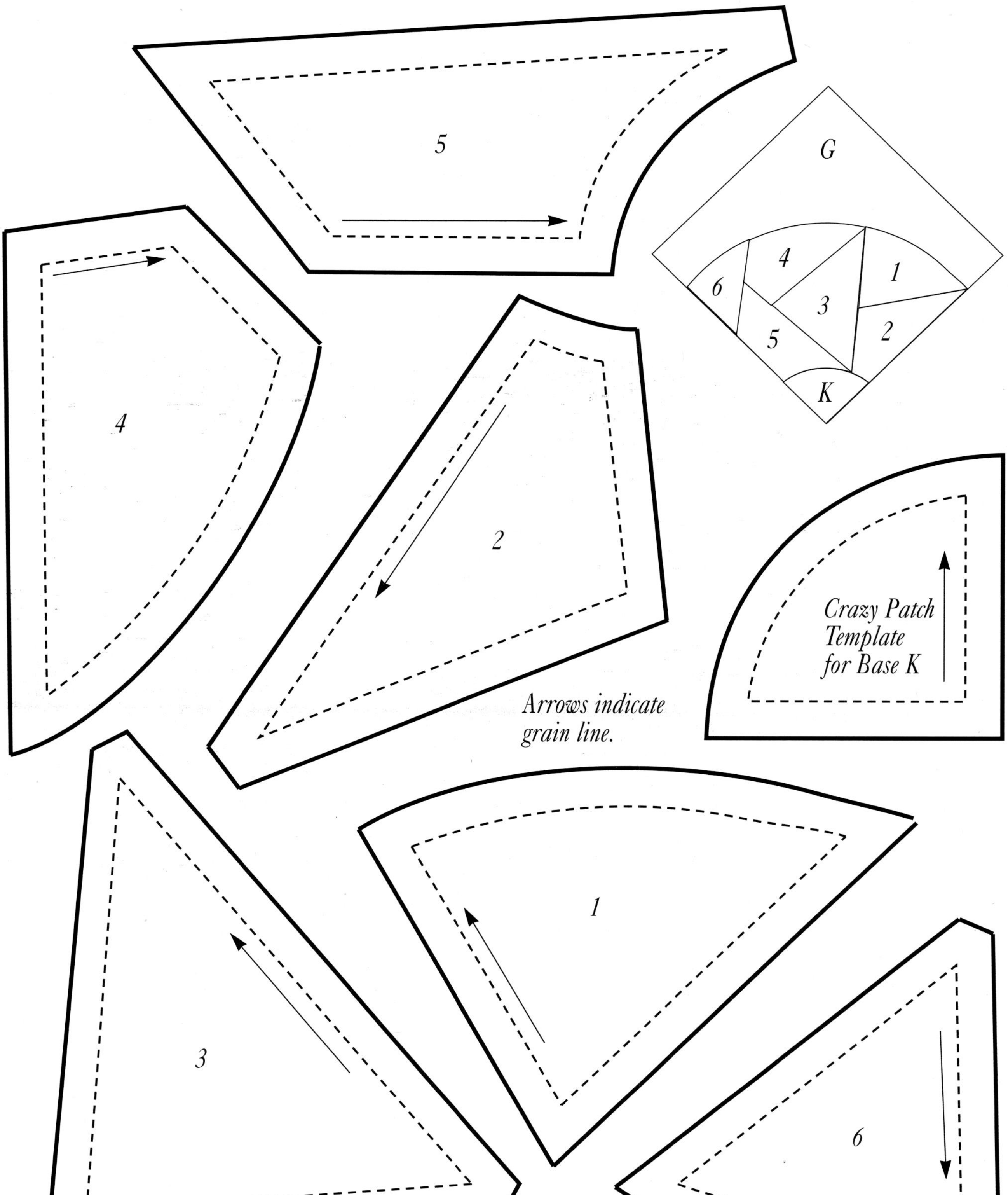

5

4

2

G

4

6

3

1

5

2

K

Crazy Patch
Template
for Base K

Arrows indicate
grain line.

3

1

6

Crazy Patch Quilting Template
for Corner Triangles

Crazy Patch Quilting Template
for Corner Squares
for Border

Crazy Patch Quilting
Template for G

6" Fan Template G

LACY FANS

The finished size is 21½" x 21½". The block size is 4".

Refer to quilt drawing and photo for color placement.

SUPPLIES

	Blocks ¼ **yard each of** **5 fabrics**	
	Border ¼ **yard**	
	Binding ¼ **yard**	
	Backing ¾ **yard**	
	Batting 26" x 26"	
	Four 8" doilies	
	⅜" wide trim **1⅞ yards**	
	Four 3" heart doilies **120 Buttons (¼" to 1")**	

CUTTING

Blocks: Cut one strip 4½" x 42" from each fabric. Open the strip and cut 16 total squares 4½" x 4½".

Border: Cut two strips 3" x 42". Open the strips and stack them. From these strips cut two strips 16½" for the sides; cut two strips 21½" for the top and bottom.

Binding: Cut three strips 1¾" x 42". Join into one long strip. From this strip cut two strips 21½" for the sides and two strips 22" for the top and bottom.

Backing: Cut one piece 26" x 26".

Doilies: Cut into quarters.

SEWING INSTRUCTIONS FOR LACY FANS

Review the Quilting Basics in Chapter 2 before you begin.

1. Place the quartered doilies on the blocks and top stitch in place. Follow the quilt drawing for placement.

2. Appliqué the heart doilies to the four corner blocks.

3. Follow the quilt drawing and arrange the blocks in rows. Follow the straight set instructions on page 33 for sewing the blocks together.

4. Follow the instructions on page 33 for adding the borders.

5. Place trim on the seam between the blocks and border. Turn under edge of trim where it meets itself. Top stitch or hand stitch in place.

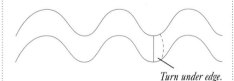

Turn under edge.

6. Follow the instructions on page 32 for stitching the buttons in place.

7. Follow the instructions on page 35 for basting the quilt.

8. This quilt was hand-quilted following the shape of the doily edge.

9. Follow the instructions on page 37 for binding the quilt.

Lacy Fans Quilt Drawing

WATERMELON SLICES

The finished size is 28" x 28". The block size is 6".

Refer to quilt drawing and photo for color placement.

SUPPLIES

CUTTING

Fan Blocks
¼ yard each of white,
2 lights, 3 darks

Cut out templates for D, E, F, and G (pages 152-153).
If each of your blocks is going to be different, cut out all of the pieces for one block at a time and set aside. If fabrics are the ones used for borders mentioned below, cut the border strips before cutting Fan patches.
Nine blocks are needed.
Center Fan Wedge E: Cut one for each block using template E.
Side Fan Wedges F: Cut two for each block using template F. Fold the fabric in half before cutting so you get a right side and a left side.
Base D: Cut one for each block using template D.
Background G: Cut one for each block using template G.

Five Borders
¼ yard each of 3 brights
and 2 mediums

First Border: Cut two strips 1¼" x 42". Open the strips and stack them. From these strips cut two strips 18½" for the sides; cut two strips 20" for the top and bottom.
Second Border: Cut two strips 1¼" x 42". Open the strips and stack them. From these strips cut two strips 20" for the sides; cut two strips 21½" for the top and bottom.
Third Border: Cut three strips 1" x 42". Join into one long strip. From this strip cut two strips 21½" for the sides; cut two strips 22½" for the top and bottom.
Fourth Border: Cut three strips 2" x 42". Join into one long strip. From this strip cut two strips 22½" for the sides; cut two strips 25½" for the top and bottom.
Fifth Border: Cut three strips 1¾" x 42". Join into one long strip. From this strip cut two strips 25½" for the sides; cut two strips 28" for the top and bottom.

Binding
¼ yard

Binding: Cut three strips 1¾" x 42". Join into one long strip. From this strip cut two strips 28" for the sides; cut two strips 28½" for the top and bottom.

Backing
1 yard

Backing: Cut one piece 32" x 32".

Batting 32" x 32"

SEWING INSTRUCTIONS FOR WATERMELON SLICES

*Review the Quilting Basics in
Chapter 2 before you begin.*

1. Follow the instructions on
page 139 to construct nine
6" Fan blocks.

2. Follow the quilt drawing
and arrange the blocks in rows.
Follow the straight set instructions
on page 33 for sewing the
blocks together.

3. Follow the instructions on
page 33 for adding the borders.

4. Follow the instructions on
page 35 for basting the quilt.

5. The stars were hand-quilted
on the surface of the quilt.
Make a template of the star on
page 152 and trace around it with
a washable or erasable pencil.

6. Follow the instructions
on page 37 for binding
the quilt.

Watermelon Slices Quilt Drawing

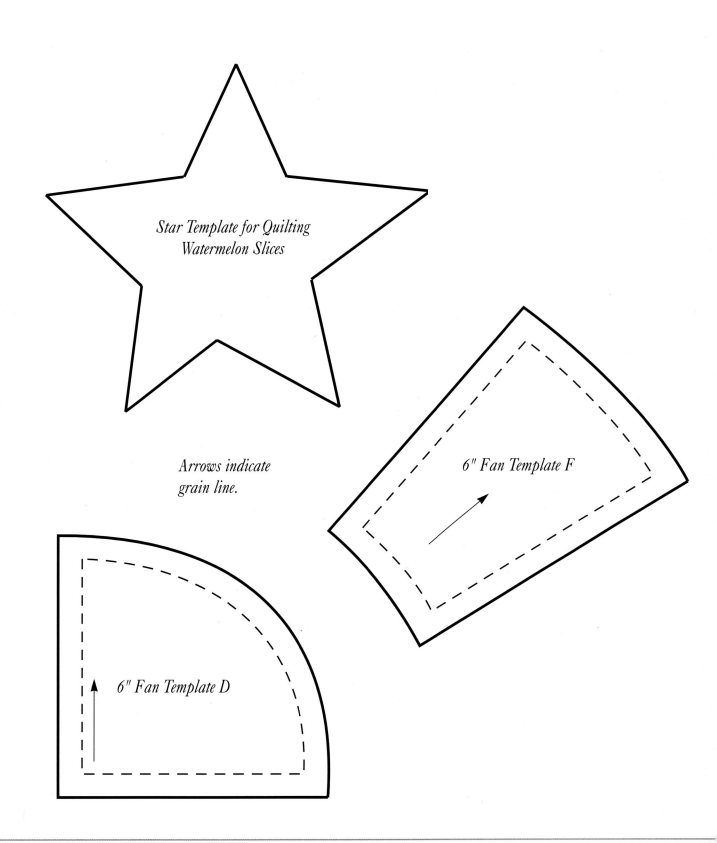

Star Template for Quilting
Watermelon Slices

Arrows indicate
grain line.

6" Fan Template F

6" Fan Template D

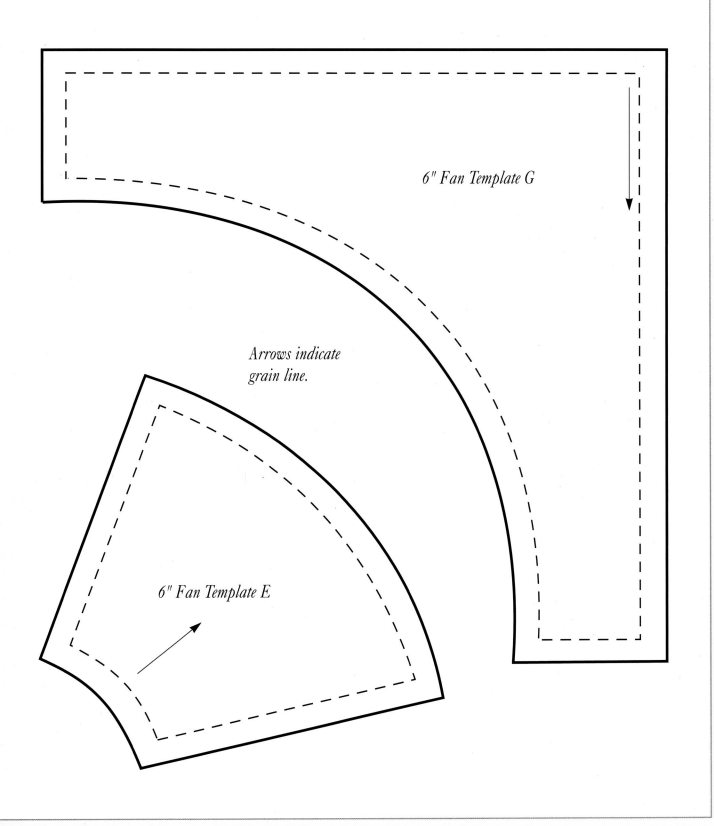

6" Fan Template G

Arrows indicate
grain line.

6" Fan Template E

Chapter Ten

BASKET QUILTS

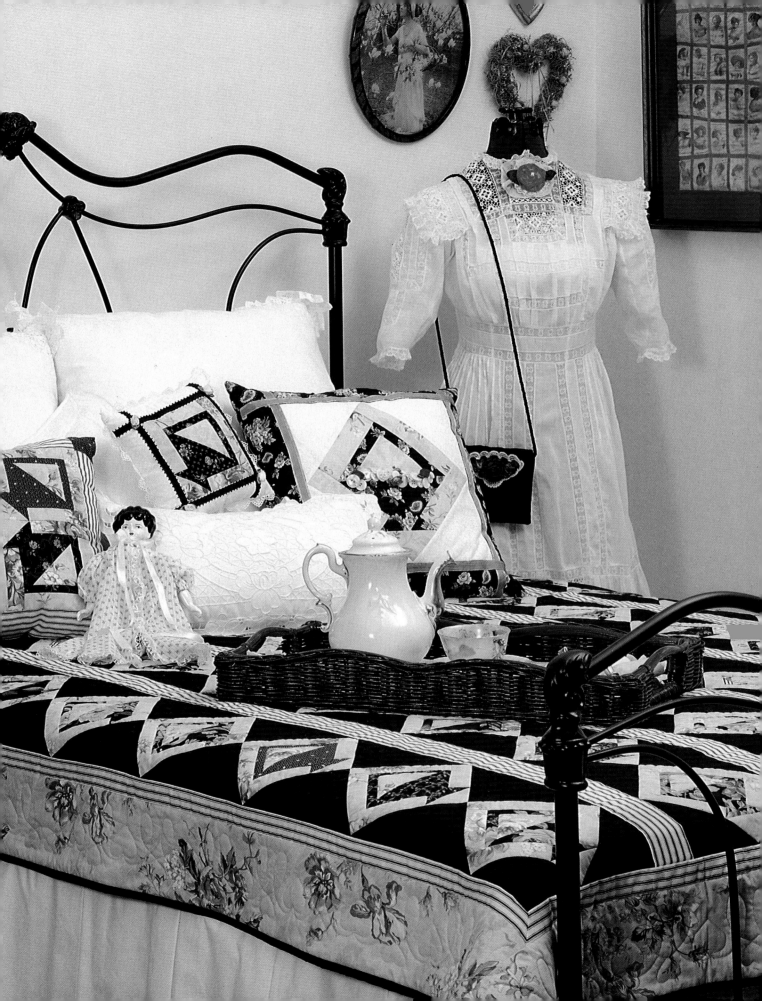

CHAPTER TEN

Basket Quilts

Basket quilts are a favorite of mine, maybe because I use a lot of baskets in my home to keep track of things. As I researched books looking for a simple basket block, I couldn't find one that didn't have an appliquéd handle. So I came up with the idea of the pieced handle, and it works really well. I like the basket in the 6" size the best because it works up easily.

The *Basket Trellis* quilt was the first one that I planned. In it, the background fabric is always the same but the baskets are different black prints. The sashing is a ticking stripe, and it was cut on the lengthwise grain so it didn't have to be pieced. It creates a lattice look in the quilt block setting.

I couldn't resist making pillows to match the quilt. I took leftover blocks from the quilt and made new arrangements. The four-block pillow design has a 12" repeat, so it can be used easily with sashing in between for a quilt. The other large pillow is a single block that is set on point with corner fabric added. I added a collection of buttons and purchased ribbon roses. The small single basket pillow is framed with fabric and decorated with ribbon. Some of my friends might use this for a decorative pincushion.

Lancaster Medallion was my next project. I've always admired the old Amish quilts with simple motifs and lots of hand quilting. That is what I tried to capture in this design.

Years ago I saw an antique basket quilt where the baskets were placed on their sides and faced each other. I was intrigued by the design and it stuck in my mind. To create the *Old-Fashioned Basket* quilt, a variety of basket fabrics needed to be collected. The background is one piece of fabric, but it could have been just as easily made of scraps. Borders were added to give extra color and to frame the quilt.

BASKET BLOCK INSTRUCTIONS

Make a pretty Basket Quilt to carry you along the easy quiltmaking path and some pillows for quick-and-easy additions. Read through all of the general instructions before you begin these projects.

Making the Basket Block

This simple Basket block has a pieced handle, which eliminates having to appliqué. The quilts and pillows use various sizes of blocks from 6" to 12". In the quilts pictured, one fabric has been used for the basket and a second for the background. Refer to the cutting guide at the right to make 6", 9", and 12" Basket blocks for your projects.

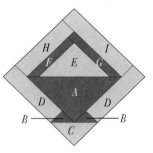

Lay the block pieces out on a flat surface next to where you are going to sew, then follow the instructions below:

1. Sew F to E, pressing seam toward F. Sew G to the other side of EF, pressing seam toward G. Trim F and G even with E.

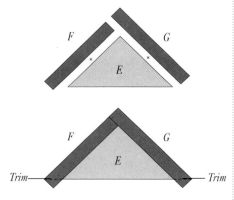

Basket Blocks

	6"	9"	12"
A: Cut one square, then cut in half diagonally.	4⅞" x 4⅞"	6⅞" x 6⅞"	8⅞" x 8⅞"
B: Cut one square, then cut in half diagonally.	1⅞" x 1⅞"	2⅜" x 2⅜"	2⅞" x 2⅞"
C: Cut one square, then cut in half diagonally.	2⅞" x 2⅞"	3⅞" x 3⅞"	4⅞" x 4⅞"
D: Cut two	1½" x 4½"	2" x 6½"	2½" x 8½"
E: Cut one square, then cut in half diagonally.	3⅞" x 3⅞"	5⅜" x 5⅜"	6⅞" x 6⅞"
F: Cut one	1" x 4¾"	1¼" x 6½"	1½" x 8¼"
G: Cut one	1" x 5½"	1¼" x 7¼"	1½" x 9¼"
H: Cut one	1½" x 4½"	2" x 6½"	2½" x 8½"
I: Cut one	1½" x 5½"	2" x 8"	2½" x 10½"

2. Sew A to EFG, pressing seam toward A. Trim excess seam allowance even with the block.

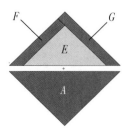

3. Sew B to D for the left and right sides of the basket. These will be mirror images of each other. Press seam toward D.

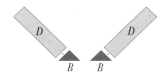

4. Follow the drawing below and add H to the basket, then I, then BD on each side. Press seams toward H and I and BD. Sew C to unit, pressing seam toward C.

BASKET TRELLIS

The finished size is 74¼" x 80½". The block size is 6".

Refer to quilt drawing and photo for color placement. Cutting directions for patches A, B, F, and G are given for a single basket block so that patches for each single basket can be cut from one fabric. Make 48 baskets.

SUPPLIES

CUTTING

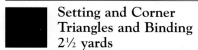

Baskets
8 to 10 fabrics totaling
1½ yards

Patch A: Cut one square 4⅞" x 4⅞". Cut in half diagonally. (This makes two basket bodies.)
Patch B: Cut one square 1⅞" x 1⅞". Cut in half diagonally.
Patch F: Cut one rectangle 1" x 4¾".
Patch G: Cut one rectangle 1" x 5½".

Basket Background and
Second Border
2¾ yards

Patch C: Cut two strips 2⅞" x 42". Cut into 24 squares 2⅞" x 2⅞". Cut in half diagonally.
Patch D: Cut 11 strips 1½" x 42". Cut into 96 rectangles 1½" x 4½".
Patch E: Cut three strips 3⅞" x 42". Cut into 24 squares 3⅞" x 3⅞". Cut in half diagonally.
Patch H: Cut six strips 1½" x 42". Cut into 48 rectangles 1½" x 4½".
Patch I: Cut seven strips 1½" x 42". Cut into 48 rectangles 1½" x 5½".
Second Border: Cut seven strips 5½" x 42". Join into one long strip. From this strip cut two strips 70½" for the sides; cut two strips 74¼" for the top and bottom.

First Border
and Sashing
2¼ yards

First Border: Cut on lengthwise grain. Cut two strips 1½" x 71¼" for the sides. Cut two strips 1½" x 65" for the top and bottom.
Sashing: Cut on lengthwise grain. Cut five strips 2¾" x 68½".

Setting and Corner
Triangles and Binding
2½ yards

Setting Triangles: Cut five strips 9¾" x 42". Cut into 20 squares 9¾" x 9¾". Cut one more 9¾" square. Cut all 21 squares into 84 quarters diagonally.
Corner Triangles: Cut two strips 5⅛" x 42". Cut into 12 squares 5⅛" x 5⅛". Cut in half diagonally to make 24 triangles.
Binding: Cut eight strips 1¾" x 42". Join two strips for each side. From these strips cut two strips 80½". Repeat joining strips for the top and bottom; cut two strips 74¾".

Backing
4¾ yards

Backing: Cut two pieces 42" x 85". Trim off the selvages and sew sections together, right sides facing, along the lengthwise grain.

Batting 79" x 85"

Sewing instructions begin on next page.

SEWING INSTRUCTIONS FOR BASKET TRELLIS

Read the Quilting Basics in Chapter 2 before you begin.

1. Follow the block construction instructions on page 157 to make 48 Basket blocks.

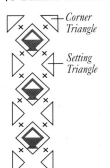

2. Arrange eight blocks vertically in a row, inserting setting and corner triangles. Sew together diagonally. Complete six vertical rows.

3. Sew a sashing strip between each row.

4. Sew on the first border using the patterns on page 34 to cut a 45° angle and following the instructions on page 34 to miter the corners.

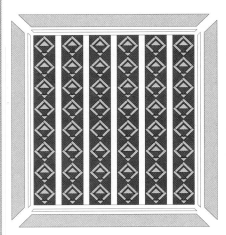

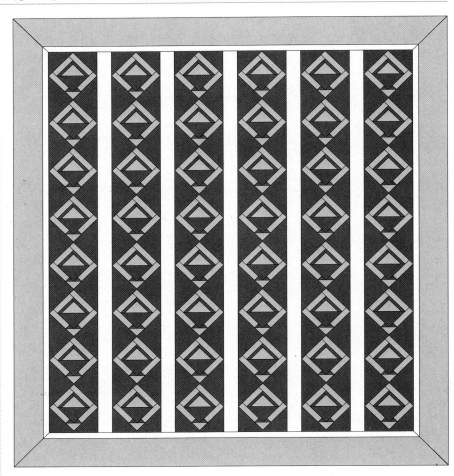

Basket Trellis Quilt Drawing

5. Follow the instructions on page 34 for adding the second mitered border.

6. Follow the instructions on page 35 for basting the quilt.

7. This quilt was machine-quilted around each basket and along the edges of the borders.

8. Follow the instructions on page 37 for binding the quilt.

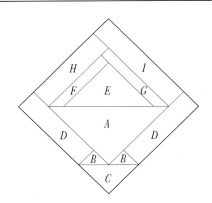

BASKET PILLOWS

From left to right:
Medallion Pillow: The finished size is 18" x 18". The block size is 9".
Single Basket Pillow: The finished size is 10" x 10". The block size is 6".
Four Baskets Pillow: The finished size is 16" x 16". The block size is 6".

MEDALLION PILLOW

Refer to pillow drawing and photo for color placement.

SUPPLIES

Basket
¼ yard

Basket Background
¼ yard

Corner Triangles
¼ yard

Border
¼ yard

Backing
⅓ **yard when using a Pillow Form**

⅝ **yard when using Fiberfill**

18" Pillow Form or 12 oz. of Fiberfill

¾" Ribbon
2⅛ yards

¾" Assorted Buttons
10 to 15

Ribbon Roses
6 to 8

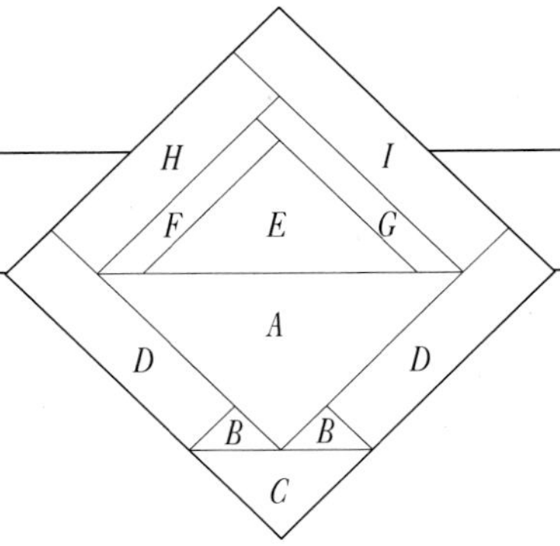

CUTTING

Patch A: Cut one square 6⅞" x 6⅞". Cut in half diagonally.
Patch B: Cut one square 2⅜" x 2⅜". Cut in half diagonally.
Patch F: Cut one rectangle 1¼" x 6½".
Patch G: Cut one rectangle 1¼" x 7¼".

Patch C: Cut one square 3⅞" x 3⅞". Cut in half diagonally.
Patch D: Cut two rectangles 2" x 6½".
Patch E: Cut one square 5⅜" x 5⅜". Cut in half diagonally.
Patch H: Cut one rectangle 2" x 6½".
Patch I: Cut one rectangle 2" x 8".

Corner Triangles: Cut two squares 7¼" x 7¼". Cut in half diagonally.

Border: Cut two strips 3½" x 42". Open the strips and stack them. From these strips cut two strips 13¼" for the sides; cut two strips 19¼" for the top and bottom.

Backing: Cut two rectangles 11¼" x 19¼" when using a pillow form. Cut one square 19¼" x 19¼" when using fiberfill.

SEWING INSTRUCTIONS FOR MEDALLION PILLOW

Read the Quilting Basics in Chapter 2 before you begin.

1. Follow the block construction instructions on page 157 to make one Basket block.

2. Add two corner triangles to opposite sides of the block, pressing toward the triangles. Repeat for remaining triangles.

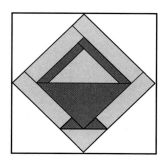

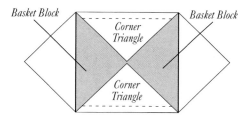

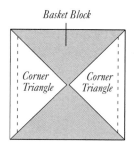

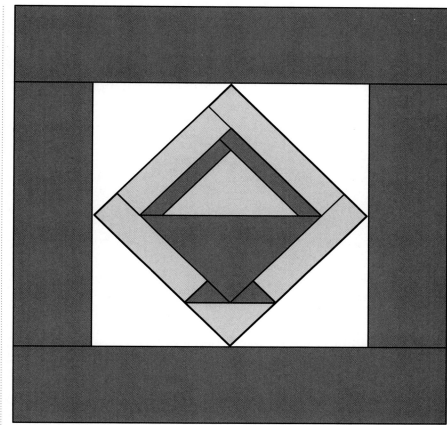

Medallion Pillow Drawing

3. Follow the instructions on page 33 for adding the border.

4. Place the ribbon at the inside edge of the border and stitch along both edges of the ribbon. Overlap ribbon at the corners. Follow the instructions on page 32 for stitching the buttons in place. Refer to the photograph for button and ribbon rose placement.

5. To stuff with fiberfill: With right sides facing, place pillow front and back together. Using ¼" seam allowance, sew edges closed, leaving a 5" opening. Turn right side out and press.

Fill with tiny wads of fiberfill. Turn the raw edges under ¼" and slip-stitch opening closed.

6. To stuff with a pillow form: Make a two-piece backing. Press one 19¼" edge under ¼". Turn the edge under ¼" again, and stitch close to the edge. Repeat for the remaining rectangle. To create a 19¼" square backing, overlap the stitched edges 3½". This overlap creates an opening for the pillow form after the backing is stitched to the front. Using a ¼" seam allowance, sew around all edges. Turn right side out and insert the pillow form.

TWO PILLOWS

Refer to pillow drawings and photo on page 161 for color. Cutting directions for patches A to I are given for a single Basket block so that patches for each single basket can be cut from a different fabric.

SUPPLIES

CUTTING

Four Baskets
6" x 16" piece of four different fabrics
Single Basket
6" x 16" piece of one fabric

Patch A: Cut one square 4⅞" x 4⅞". Cut in half diagonally.
Patch B: Cut one square 1⅞" x 1⅞". Cut in half diagonally.
Patch F: Cut one rectangle 1" x 4¾".
Patch G: Cut one rectangle 1" x 5½".

Four Baskets Background
⅓ yard
Single Basket Background
⅛ yard

Patch C: Cut one square 2⅞" x 2⅞". Cut in half diagonally.
Patch D: Cut two rectangles 1½" x 4½".
Patch E: Cut one square 3⅞" x 3⅞". Cut in half diagonally.
Patch H: Cut one rectangle 1½" x 4½".
Patch I: Cut one rectangle 1½" x 5½".

Four Baskets
Corner Posts
⅛ yard

Corner Posts: Cut four squares 2½" x 2½".

Four Baskets Border
and Backing
½ yard

Border: Cut four strips 2½" x 12½".
Backing: Cut two pieces 10½" x 16½" when using a pillow form or cut one square 16½" x 16½" when using fiberfill.

Single Basket Border
and Backing
½ yard

Border: Cut one strip 2½" x 42". Open the strip and cut two strips 6½" for the sides; cut two strips 10½" for the top and bottom.
Backing: Cut two pieces 10½" x 7½" when using a pillow form or cut one square 10½" x 10½" when using fiberfill.

16" Pillow Form or
10 oz. of Fiberfill for
Four Baskets Pillow

10" Pillow Form or
8 oz. of Fiberfill for
Single Basket Pillow

For Single Basket Pillow:
½"-wide Ribbon 1¼ yards

Lace 1¼ yards

4 Ribbon Roses

SEWING INSTRUCTIONS FOR BASKET PILLOWS

Review the Quilting Basics in Chapter 2 before you begin.

FOUR BASKETS PILLOW

1. Follow the block construction directions on page 157 to make four blocks.

2. Refer to the pillow drawing for placement. Follow the straight set instructions on page 33 for sewing the blocks together.

3. Sew one border strip to two opposite sides of the Four Baskets block. Sew a corner post to each end of the two remaining border strips, then sew the strips to top and bottom of pillow.

4. Follow the instructions in Step 5 or Step 6 on page 163 for finishing the pillow.

Four Baskets Pillow Drawing

SINGLE BASKET PILLOW

1. Follow the block construction instructions on page 157 to make a Basket block.

2. Follow the instructions on page 33 for adding the border.

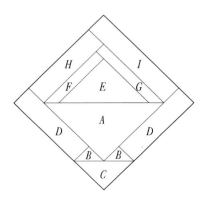

3. Place ribbon at the inside edge of the borders and stitch on both sides of the ribbon. Overlap ribbons at the inner corners. Hand stitch roses atop ribbon intersections at inner corners, referring to the photograph on page 161.

4. Follow the instructions in Step 5 or Step 6 on page 163 for finishing the pillow.

5. Slip-stitch lace to pillow edges, easing it around the corners.

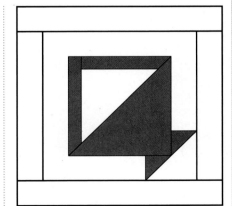

Single Basket Pillow Drawing

LANCASTER MEDALLION

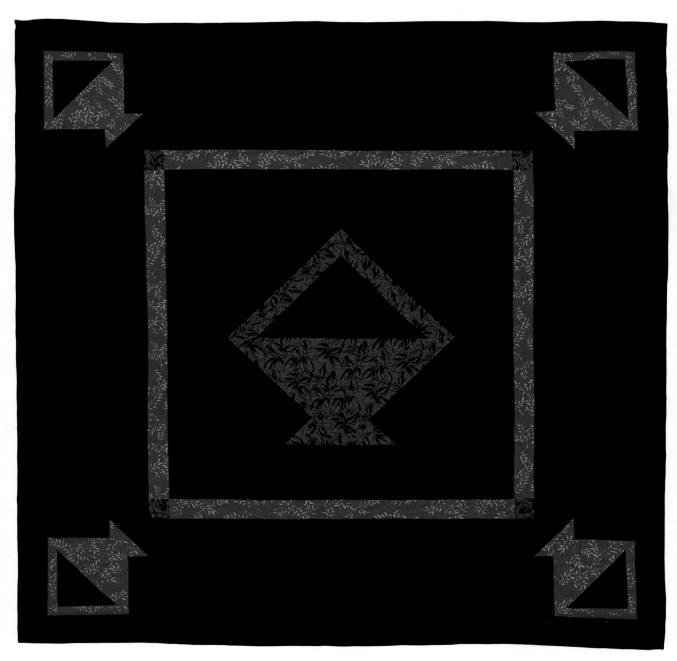

The finished size is 31½" x 31½". Block sizes are 12" and 6".

Refer to quilt drawing and photo for color placement.

SUPPLIES

CUTTING

One 12" Basket and Corner Posts ¼ yard	**Patch A:** Cut one square 8⅞" x 8⅞". Cut in half diagonally. **Patch B:** Cut one square 2⅞" x 2⅞". Cut in half diagonally. **Patch F:** Cut one rectangle 1½" x 8¼". **Patch G:** Cut one rectangle 1½" x 9¼".
Four 6" Baskets and First Border ¼ yard	**Corner Posts:** Cut four squares 1½" x 1½". **Patch A:** Cut two squares 4⅞" x 4⅞". Cut in half diagonally. **Patch B:** Cut four squares 1⅞" x 1⅞". Cut in half diagonally. **Patch F:** Cut four rectangles 1" x 4¾". **Patch G:** Cut four rectangles 1" x 5½". **First Border:** Cut two strips 1½" x 42". Open the strips and stack them. From these strips cut four strips 17½".
Background, Corner Triangles, Second Border, and Binding 1⅛ yards	*Background for 12" Basket:* **Patch C:** Cut one square 4⅞" x 4⅞". Cut in half diagonally. **Patch D:** Cut two rectangles 2½" x 8½". **Patch E:** Cut one square 6⅞" x 6⅞". Cut in half diagonally. **Patch H:** Cut one rectangle 2½" x 8½". **Patch I:** Cut one rectangle 2½" x 10½". *Background for 6" Baskets:* **Patch C:** Cut two squares 2⅞" x 2⅞". Cut in half diagonally. **Patch D:** Cut eight rectangles 1½" x 4½". **Patch E:** Cut two squares 3⅞" x 3⅞". Cut in half diagonally. **Patch H:** Cut four rectangles 1½" x 4½". **Patch I:** Cut four rectangles 1½" x 5½". **Corner Triangles:** Cut two squares 9⅜" x 9⅜". Cut in half diagonally. **Second Border:** Cut two strips 6½" x 42". Open the strips and stack them. Cut four strips 19½". **Binding:** Cut four strips 1¾" x 42". From these strips cut two strips 31½" for the sides; cut two strips 32" for the top and bottom.
Backing 1 yard	**Backing:** Cut one piece 36" x 36".
Batting 36" x 36"	

Sewing instructions begin on next page.

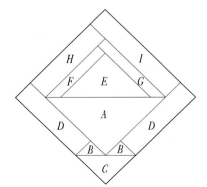

SEWING INSTRUCTIONS FOR LANCASTER MEDALLION

Review the Quilting Basics in Chapter 2 before you begin.

1. Follow the block construction instructions on page 157 to make one 12" block for the center and four 6" blocks for the borders.

2. Attach the corner triangles to the 12" center block.

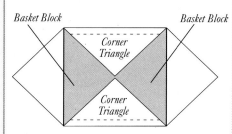

Basket Block

Corner Triangle   Corner Triangle

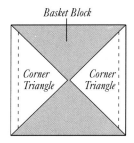

Basket Block   Basket Block

Corner Triangle

Corner Triangle

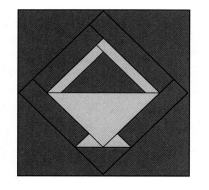

Lancaster Medallion Quilt Drawing

3. Sew border strips to two opposite sides of the center block. Sew a corner post to each end of the remaining border strips, then sew strips to top and bottom of center block.

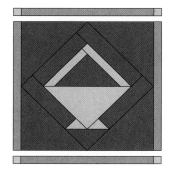

4. Follow the same procedure for adding the second border, using 6" Basket blocks as the corner posts.

5. Follow the instructions on page 35 for basting the quilt.

6. This quilt was machine-quilted. Find quilting designs that you like for the baskets and corner triangles. Trace and quilt. A scallop was quilted in the first border of the pictured quilt, and the second border was quilted diagonally on a 2" grid.

7. Follow the instructions on page 37 for binding the quilt.

OLD-FASHIONED BASKETS

The finished size is 52" x 60½". The block size is 6".

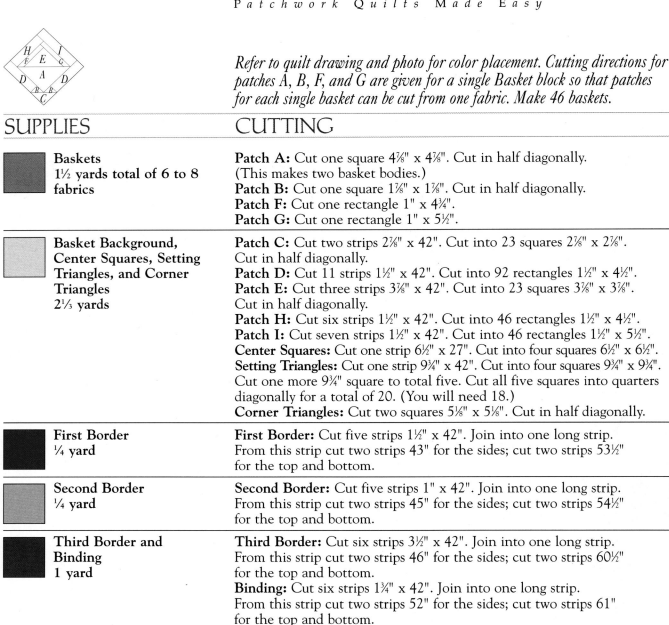

Refer to quilt drawing and photo for color placement. Cutting directions for patches A, B, F, and G are given for a single Basket block so that patches for each single basket can be cut from one fabric. Make 46 baskets.

SUPPLIES

CUTTING

Baskets
1½ yards total of 6 to 8 fabrics

Patch A: Cut one square 4⅞" x 4⅞". Cut in half diagonally. (This makes two basket bodies.)
Patch B: Cut one square 1⅞" x 1⅞". Cut in half diagonally.
Patch F: Cut one rectangle 1" x 4¾".
Patch G: Cut one rectangle 1" x 5½".

Basket Background, Center Squares, Setting Triangles, and Corner Triangles
2⅓ yards

Patch C: Cut two strips 2⅞" x 42". Cut into 23 squares 2⅞" x 2⅞". Cut in half diagonally.
Patch D: Cut 11 strips 1½" x 42". Cut into 92 rectangles 1½" x 4½".
Patch E: Cut three strips 3⅞" x 42". Cut into 23 squares 3⅞" x 3⅞". Cut in half diagonally.
Patch H: Cut six strips 1½" x 42". Cut into 46 rectangles 1½" x 4½".
Patch I: Cut seven strips 1½" x 42". Cut into 46 rectangles 1½" x 5½".
Center Squares: Cut one strip 6½" x 27". Cut into four squares 6½" x 6½".
Setting Triangles: Cut one strip 9¾" x 42". Cut into four squares 9¾" x 9¾". Cut one more 9¾" square to total five. Cut all five squares into quarters diagonally for a total of 20. (You will need 18.)
Corner Triangles: Cut two squares 5⅛" x 5⅛". Cut in half diagonally.

First Border
¼ yard

First Border: Cut five strips 1½" x 42". Join into one long strip. From this strip cut two strips 43" for the sides; cut two strips 53½" for the top and bottom.

Second Border
¼ yard

Second Border: Cut five strips 1" x 42". Join into one long strip. From this strip cut two strips 45" for the sides; cut two strips 54½" for the top and bottom.

Third Border and Binding
1 yard

Third Border: Cut six strips 3½" x 42". Join into one long strip. From this strip cut two strips 46" for the sides; cut two strips 60½" for the top and bottom.
Binding: Cut six strips 1¾" x 42". Join into one long strip. From this strip cut two strips 52" for the sides; cut two strips 61" for the top and bottom.

Backing
3⅛ yards

Backing: Cut two pieces 42" x 56". Trim off the selvages and sew sections together, right sides facing, along the lengthwise grain.

Batting 56" x 65"

SEWING INSTRUCTIONS FOR OLD-FASHIONED BASKETS

Review the Quilting Basics in Chapter 2 before you begin.

1. Follow the block construction instructions on page 157 to make 46 Basket blocks.

2. Refer to the quilt drawing for block layout, and insert the setting triangles and corners. Follow the diagonal set instructions on page 33 for sewing the blocks together.

3. Follow the instructions on page 33 for adding three borders.

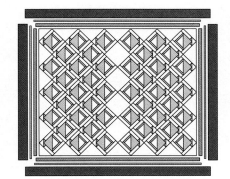

4. Follow the instructions on page 35 for basting the quilt.

5. This quilt was machine-quilted along the seam lines between the baskets and along the border. Trace a basket shape in the center blocks and quilt.

6. Follow the instructions on page 37 for binding the quilt.

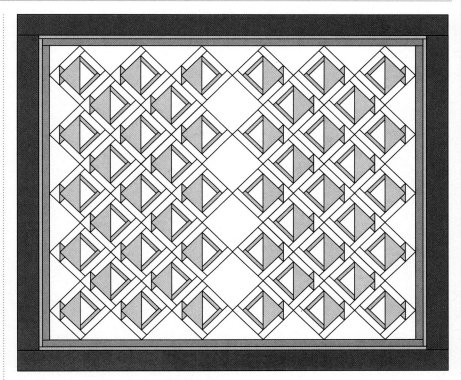

Old-Fashioned Baskets Quilt Drawing

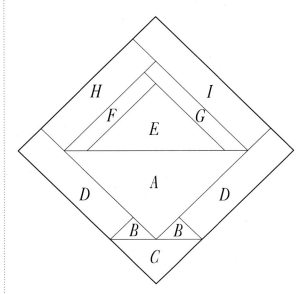

Chapter Eleven

LOG CABIN
QUILTS

CHAPTER ELEVEN

Log Cabin Quilts

Log Cabin quilts are an all-time favorite. I sell more Log Cabin quilts in my store than any other, and one can easily see how the block is constructed. Log Cabin quilts have a country sort of appearance because of their design, but they can be made to look contemporary or Victorian with different fabric selections.

Traditionally, the center block was red or a shade of red like rust, wine, or rose. It symbolized the hearth of the home. The logs (strips) were then stacked around the center block—half were light and half were dark. There are many variations of the Log Cabin block. I have included some very easy, traditional block arrangements, and then included some variations to challenge you like the *Autumn Pines* and *Mountain Sunrise*. These quilts will take a little more time in the planning process, but once you start stitching, they are made with the basic Log Cabin technique.

Indian Summer is made of a flannel plaid and solids. It is so soft to touch that you want to crawl right under it. Two of the sides are pieced with the same wine-colored fabric creating a zigzag appearance. Notice how the cream logs create a framing effect. If you place the lightest value in the same place each time, you will get this effect. The gold center fabric is a calico, not a flannel.

Jean Humenansky of the Country Peddler loaned me her off-set Log Cabin quilt made with 1930s fabric. If you look closely, you will see a great variety of fabrics that look like the old house dresses of that period. The strips on the light sides are narrower than the colored strips, which creates a new pattern. The strip-pieced border is made up of all the leftover colored fabric and makes a nice frame.

Mountain Sunrise is an "icy hot" collection of colors. A variety of fabrics was used in each color family to create texture, but you could use the same fabric throughout each color family if you like. Beginning with the dark, deep magentas in the center and ending with them in the border helps to give the design unity. This Log Cabin setting is called Barn Raising.

Autumn Pines was chosen for the cover of this book. It began with a print that included browns, golds, greens, rusts, and a touch of purple. When it was completed, everyone was moved by the richness of the colors. This combination sings because the touch of purple is unexpected and adds richness to a somewhat predictable palette. Several years ago, our local guild, the East of the Cascades Quilters, made a raffle quilt in the same setting. It was one of my favorites so I wanted to make another one. My friend, Ursula Searles, and I planned it, and then she put it together. The pieced tree border was inspired by Kathy Sanders, a quiltmaker in Washington.

LOG CABIN BLOCK INSTRUCTIONS

Along your easy quiltmaking path look for the Log Cabin with its traditional red hearth square. Then personalize it with your own color schemes. Read through all of the general instructions before you begin these projects.

Log Cabin Block Construction

Each of the quilts in this chapter uses the same technique for block construction even though the blocks themselves are different. Be sure to refer to the block drawing for the quilt you are making as you follow the general instructions here for construction.

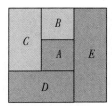 The block is constructed of a center square A with strip B added, then strip C, and so on. Follow the letters with your eyes, and you will see that the strips (logs) are added in a circle.

Two of the Log Cabin sides are one color family, and the other two sides are a contrasting color. With this contrast, a definite diagonal line forms from corner to corner across the block. You can play with this diagonal design and arrange the blocks like any of the quilts in this chapter.

Cutting Secrets

The Log Cabin block consists of strips that are cut into different lengths. Once the 42" strips are cut, open them and stack them three or four deep. Trim off the selvages at one end and cut the length indicated for A, B, and so forth. Use little sticky notes to label the piles. Arrange the piles in the order they will be used in the block. This pre-organization will save you time in the end.

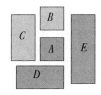

Construction

1. Pick up A and B, placing right sides together and stitch. As you near the end of the seam, pick up another A and B and feed in as you finish the first, chaining all of the A's and B's together. If you are using a variety of fabrics for any of the B's, switch fabrics as you move along.

A is under B

2. Clip the threads between the sewn pairs, and press the seam allowances toward B.

3. Pick up C and place AB on top of it. Stitch all of the AB's to C, chaining them as before.

C is under B A

4. Clip threads. Press the seam allowances toward C.

5. Pick up D and repeat as above. Continue chaining.

D is under C B A

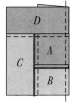
6. Pick up E and repeat as above. Continue chaining.

E is under D C B A

Now you have created one round (gone around the center block). The colors are set with lights on two sides and darks on two sides. This will alert you to which color to pick up next.

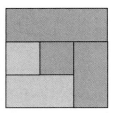 Here is an easy rule to follow: The last row you stitched will always be at the top when you add the next strip. Always press seams toward the outside of the block.

175

INDIAN SUMMER

The finished size is 63½" x 87½". The block size is 12".

Refer to quilt drawing and photo for color placement. Refer to block illustration as you cut the strips. Use sticky notes to label each stacks of logs. Once the 42" strips are cut, open them and stack three to four deep. Cut the lengths indicated.

SUPPLIES

CUTTING

Patch A
¼ yard

Patch A: Cut two strips 3½" x 42". Open the strips and stack them. Cut into 24 squares 3½" x 3½".

Light Patches B & C, First Border, Binding
1⅛ yards

Patches B and C: Cut five strips 2" x 42". Open the strips and stack them. Cut 24 strips 3½" for Patch B and 24 strips 5" for Patch C.
First Border: Cut six strips 2" x 42". Join into one long strip. From this strip cut two strips 72½" for the sides; cut two strips 51½" for the top and bottom.
Binding: Cut eight strips 1¼" x 42". Join into one long strip. From this strip cut two strips 63½" for the sides; cut two strips 88" for the top and bottom.

Light Patches F & G
⅝ yard

Patches F and G: Cut nine strips 2" x 42". Open the strips and stack them. Cut 24 strips 6½" for Patch F and 24 strips 8" for Patch G.

Light Patches J & K, Second Border
2¼ yards

Patches J and K: Cut 14 strips 2" x 42". Open the strips and stack them. Cut 24 strips 9½" for Patch J and 24 strips 11" for Patch K.
Second Border: Cut seven strips 6½" x 42". Join into one long strip. From this strip cut two strips 75½" for the sides; cut two strips 63½" for the top and bottom.

Dark Patches D, E, H, I, L & M,
2 yards

Patches D, E, H, I, L, and M: Cut 34 strips 2" x 42". Open the strips and stack them. Cut 24 for each of the following lengths: D = 5"; E = 6½"; H = 8"; I = 9½"; L = 11"; M = 12½".

Backing
5¼ yards

Backing: Cut two pieces 42" x 92". Trim off the selvages and sew sections together, right sides facing, along the lengthwise grain.

Batting 67" x 92"

Embroidery floss, lightweight yarn, or heavy cotton thread to match Patch A for tying the quilt

Sewing instructions begin on next page.

SEWING INSTRUCTIONS FOR INDIAN SUMMER

Review the Quilting Basics in Chapter 2 before you begin.

1. Follow the block construction instructions on page 175 and make 24 Log Cabin blocks.

2. Follow the quilt schematic and arrange the blocks in rows. Follow the straight set instructions on page 33 for sewing the blocks together.

3. Follow the instructions on page 33 for adding the borders.

4. Follow the instructions on page 35 for basting the quilt.

5. This quilt is machine-quilted between the blocks and tied in the center squares (Patch A).

6. To tie the quilt, use lightweight yarn, embroidery floss, or heavy cotton thread. Cut a 6" length. Use an embroidery needle, and take a stitch where you want the quilt to be secured, bringing the thread up to the right side. Tie a square knot. Trim the ends leaving ½" tails.

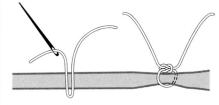

7. Follow the instructions on page 37 for binding the quilt.

Indian Summer Quilt Drawing

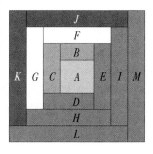

1930s LOG CABIN

The finished size is 39¾" x 50½". The block size is 5⅜".

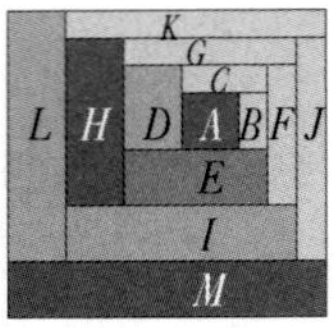

Refer to quilt drawing and photo for color placement. Refer to block illustration as you cut out the strips. Use sticky notes to label each stack of logs. Once the 42" strips are cut, open them, and stack three or four deep. Then cut the lengths indicated.

SUPPLIES

CUTTING

Variety of Light Pinks for Log Cabin, First Border, Binding to total 1¼ yards	**Lights:** Cut 24 strips 1⅛" x 42". Open strips and stack them. Cut 48 each of the following lengths: B = 1⅜"; C = 2"; F = 2⅞"; G = 3½"; J = 4⅜"; K = 5". **First Border:** Cut four strips 1⅛" x 42". Join into one long strip. From this strip cut two strips 43½" for the sides; cut two strips 34" for the top and bottom. **Binding:** Cut five strips 1¾" x 42". Join into one long strip. From this strip cut two strips 50½" for the sides; cut two strips 41¼" for the top and bottom.
Variety of Dark Prints for Log Cabin, Second Border to total 2¼ yards	**Darks:** Cut 30 strips 1⅜" x 42". Open strips and stack them. Cut 48 each of the following lengths: D = 2"; E = 2⅞"; H = 3½"; I = 4⅜"; L = 5"; M = 5⅞". **Second Border:** Cut 16 strips 1⅜" x 42" from a variety of fabrics. Cut into 3⅜" pieces. Stitch 51 pieces together twice for the sides and 45 together for the top and bottom.
Patch A ⅛ yard	**Patch A:** Cut two strips 1⅜" x 42". Cut into 48 squares 1⅜" x 1⅜".
Backing 1½ yards	**Backing:** Cut one piece 42" x 55". If your fabric is just 42" wide, center the quilt top on the backing.
Batting 44" x 55"	

SEWING INSTRUCTIONS FOR 1930s LOG CABIN

Review the Quilting Basics in Chapter 2 before you begin.

1. Follow the block construction instructions on page 175. Make 48 Log Cabin blocks.

2. Follow the quilt drawing and arrange the rows. Follow the straight set instructions on page 33 for sewing the blocks together.

3. Follow the instructions on page 33 for adding the borders.

4. Follow the instructions on page 35 for basting the quilt.

5. This quilt was first machine-quilted around each block and along the borders. Then a half circle design was stitched through the dark print side of the Log Cabin blocks. Make a template of the shape from the pattern on page 182. Then lightly trace the shape with a washable pencil and machine-quilt it.

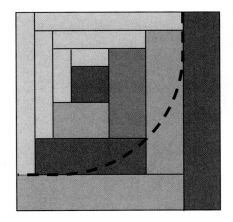

6. Follow the instructions on page 37 for binding the quilt.

1930s Log Cabin Quilt Drawing

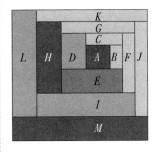

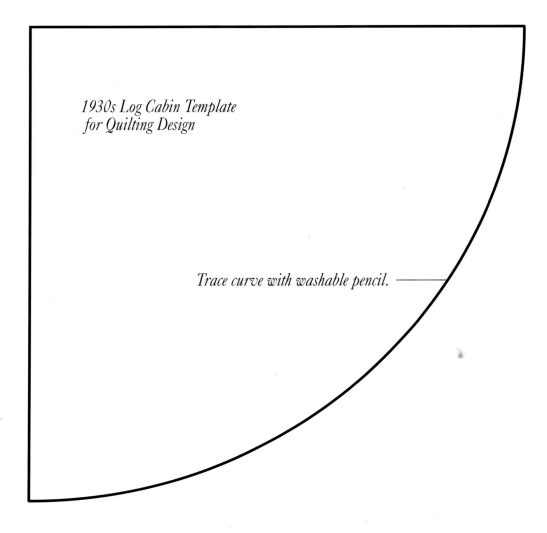

*1930s Log Cabin Template
for Quilting Design*

Trace curve with washable pencil.

AUTUMN PINES

The finished size is 82½" x 94½". The block size is 11¼".

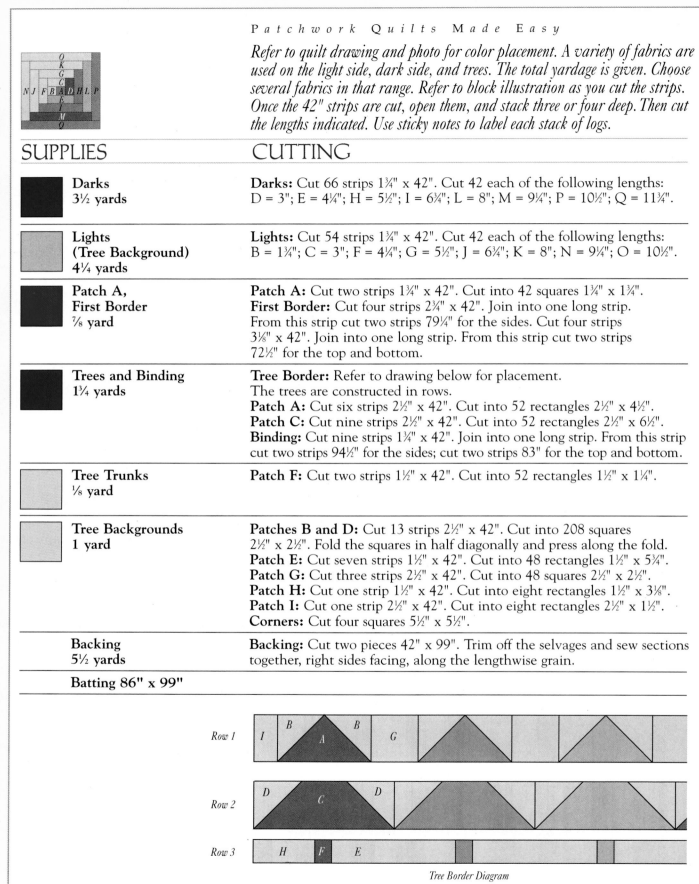

Refer to quilt drawing and photo for color placement. A variety of fabrics are used on the light side, dark side, and trees. The total yardage is given. Choose several fabrics in that range. Refer to block illustration as you cut the strips. Once the 42" strips are cut, open them, and stack three or four deep. Then cut the lengths indicated. Use sticky notes to label each stack of logs.

SUPPLIES

Darks
3½ yards

**Lights
(Tree Background)**
4¼ yards

**Patch A,
First Border**
⅞ yard

Trees and Binding
1¾ yards

Tree Trunks
⅛ yard

Tree Backgrounds
1 yard

Backing
5½ yards

Batting 86" x 99"

CUTTING

Darks: Cut 66 strips 1¾" x 42". Cut 42 each of the following lengths: D = 3"; E = 4¼"; H = 5½"; I = 6¾"; L = 8"; M = 9¼"; P = 10½"; Q = 11¾".

Lights: Cut 54 strips 1¾" x 42". Cut 42 each of the following lengths: B = 1¾"; C = 3"; F = 4¼"; G = 5½"; J = 6¾"; K = 8"; N = 9¼"; O = 10½".

Patch A: Cut two strips 1¾" x 42". Cut into 42 squares 1¾" x 1¾".
First Border: Cut four strips 2¾" x 42". Join into one long strip. From this strip cut two strips 79¼" for the sides. Cut four strips 3⅛" x 42". Join into one long strip. From this strip cut two strips 72½" for the top and bottom.

Tree Border: Refer to drawing below for placement. The trees are constructed in rows.
Patch A: Cut six strips 2½" x 42". Cut into 52 rectangles 2½" x 4½".
Patch C: Cut nine strips 2½" x 42". Cut into 52 rectangles 2½" x 6½".
Binding: Cut nine strips 1¾" x 42". Join into one long strip. From this strip cut two strips 94½" for the sides; cut two strips 83" for the top and bottom.

Patch F: Cut two strips 1½" x 42". Cut into 52 rectangles 1½" x 1¼".

Patches B and D: Cut 13 strips 2½" x 42". Cut into 208 squares 2½" x 2½". Fold the squares in half diagonally and press along the fold.
Patch E: Cut seven strips 1½" x 42". Cut into 48 rectangles 1½" x 5¾".
Patch G: Cut three strips 2½" x 42". Cut into 48 squares 2½" x 2½".
Patch H: Cut one strip 1½" x 42". Cut into eight rectangles 1½" x 3⅛".
Patch I: Cut one strip 2½" x 42". Cut into eight rectangles 2½" x 1½".
Corners: Cut four squares 5½" x 5½".

Backing: Cut two pieces 42" x 99". Trim off the selvages and sew sections together, right sides facing, along the lengthwise grain.

Tree Border Diagram

SEWING INSTRUCTIONS FOR AUTUMN PINES

Review the Quilting Basics in Chapter 2 before you begin.

1. Follow the block construction instructions on page 175. Make 42 Log Cabin blocks.

2. Refer to the quilt drawing and arrange in rows. Follow the straight set instructions on page 33 for sewing the blocks together.

3. Follow the instructions on page 33 for adding the first border.

4. In the second border, there are 14 trees on each side and 12 trees on the top and bottom. The tree borders are constructed in three rows.

5. *Row 1 of the Tree Border:*
Using Patch A and Patch B, follow the instructions on page 73 and construct 52 double half-square triangles. Row 1 consists of 14 AB's, 13 G's, and two I's for each side border and 12 AB's, 11 G's and 2 I's for each top and bottom border. Add AB to G to AB and continue alternating them until you have sewn the required amount for each border. Be sure that all AB's are positioned in the same direction. Sew one I to each end of Row 1.

6. *Row 2 of the Tree Border:*
Using Patch C and Patch D, follow the instructions on page 73 and construct 52 double half-square triangles, which are wider than the AB patches in Row 1. Sew 14 CD's for the side borders and 12 Patch CD's for the top and bottom borders. Be sure that all CD's are positioned in the same direction.

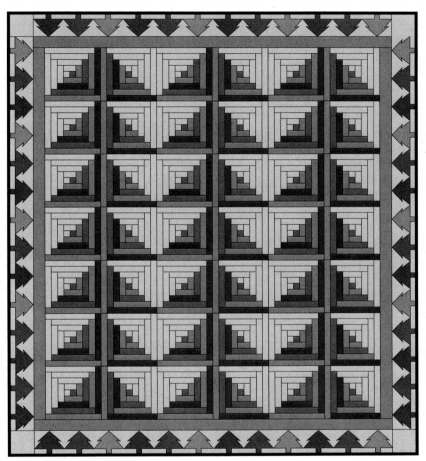

Autumn Pines Quilt Drawing

7. *Row 3 of the Tree Border:*
Sew 14 F's, 13 E's, and two H's for each side border and 12 F's, 11 E's and 2 H's for each top and bottom border. Add F to E to F and continue alternating them until you have sewn the required amount for each border. Sew one H to each end of Row 3.

8. Sew Row 1, Row 2, and Row 3 together. Follow the instructions on page 33 for adding the tree borders.

9. Follow the instructions on page 35 for basting the quilt.

10. This quilt was machine-quilted in-the-ditch.

11. Follow the instructions on page 37 for binding the quilt.

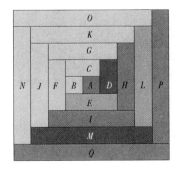

MOUNTAIN SUNRISE

The finished size is 75½" x 75½". The block size is 6¾".

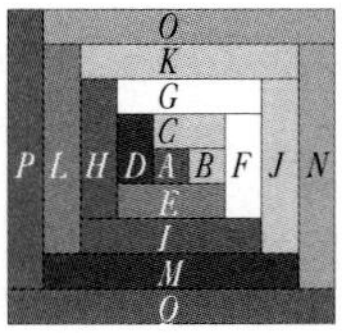

Refer to quilt drawing and photo for color placement. Refer to block illustration as you cut the strips. Use sticky notes to label the stacks of logs.

SUPPLIES

In this quilt, each of the color families consists of a variety of fabrics. Look at the pink round. You see mostly lights, but the deeper pinks help define the blocks. For easy reference the colors of the quilt have been used in this chart. You may substitute your own colors.

CUTTING

Cut the following numbers of 1¼" x 42" strips from all of the Log Cabin fabrics: Magenta = 16; Pink = 20; Teal = 48; Aqua = 31; Blue = 50; Magenta/purple = 13. Cut lengths for one set of blocks at a time and construct those. Then do the next set of blocks. The letters indicate the lengths to be cut from each color: A & B = 1¼"; C & D = 2"; E & F = 2¾"; G & H = 3½"; I & J = 4¼"; K & L = 5"; M & N = 5¾"; O & P = 6½"; Q = 7¼".

	no. of Blocks	Cutting
Magentas **⅝ yard total**	**4 Magenta**	Magenta: Cut four each of A-Q.
Pinks **¾ yard total**	**8 Mag./Pink**	Pink: Cut eight each of A, B, C, F, G, J, K, N, O. Magenta: Cut eight each of D, E, H, I, L, M, P, Q.
Teals **1¾ yards total**	**12 Pink/Teal**	Pink: Cut 12 each of A, B, C, F, G, J, K, N, O. Teal: Cut 12 each of D, E, H, I, L, M, P, Q.
Aquas **1⅛ yards total**	**16 Teal** **20 Teal/Aqua**	Teal: Cut 16 each of A-Q. Aqua: Cut 20 each of A, B, C, F, G, J, K, N, O. Teal: Cut 20 each of D, E, H, I, L, M, P, Q.
Blues **1⅞ yards total**	**16 Aqua/Blue**	Aqua: Cut 16 each of A, B, C, F, G, J, K, N, O. Blue: Cut 16 each of D, E, H, I, L, M, P, Q.
Dark Magentas/Purples **½ yard total**	**12 Blue** **12 Blue/ Mag./Purple**	Blue: Cut 12 each of A-Q. Blue: Cut 12 each of A, B, C, F, G, J, K, N, O. Mag./Purple: Cut 12 each of D, E, H, I, L, M, P, Q.
Border **1 yard**	**Border:** Cut eight strips 4¼" x 42". Join into one long strip. From this strip cut four S strips 32½" for the sides; cut four T strips 36¼" for the top and bottom.	
Binding **½ yard**	**Binding:** Cut eight strips 1¾" x 42". Join into one long strip. From this strip cut two strips 75½" for the sides; cut two strips 76" for the top and bottom.	
Border Inset **⅜ yard**	**Border Inset:** Cut two strips 4¼" x 42". Open the strips and stack them. Cut four R strips 14¾".	
Backing **4½ yards**	**Backing:** Cut two pieces 42" x 80". Trim off the selvages and sew sections together, right sides facing, along the lengthwise grain.	
Batting 80" x 80"		

Sewing instructions begin on next page.

SEWING INSTRUCTIONS FOR MOUNTAIN SUNRISE

Review the Quilting Basics in Chapter 2 before you begin.

1. Construct the blocks in color groups.

2. Refer to the photo and arrange the blocks in rows. Follow the straight set instructions on page 33 for sewing the blocks together.

3. You will need to cut a 45° angle on the strips for the borders. Stack two S strips right sides together. Place the triangle template on page 189 on one end and cut the angle to make an S and an S reversed (Sr). Repeat. Also, repeat for T, making two T's and two T's reversed (Tr).

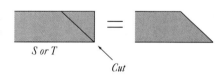

S or T = *Cut*

4. For R, stack four strips. Use the template to cut an angle at each end.

Cut R

Cut

5. Sew border patches together as shown. Follow the instructions on page 33 for adding the borders.

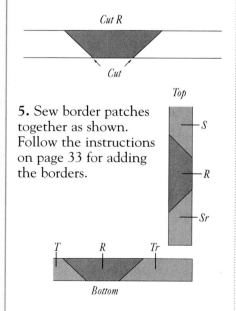

Top
—S
—R
—Sr
T   *R*   *Tr*
Bottom

Mountain Sunrise Quilt Drawing

6. Make the template for the quilting design on page 189. Trace it onto the light section of the blocks using a washable marking pencil.

7. Follow the instructions on page 35 for basting the quilt.

8. This quilt was machine-quilted between the blocks and along the border. Also, quilt on the lines marked in Step 6.

9. Follow the instructions on page 37 for binding the quilt.

❖ *This color combination uses an "echo" color technique. The light version is the echo of the darker one. This contrast adds interest to the color palette.*

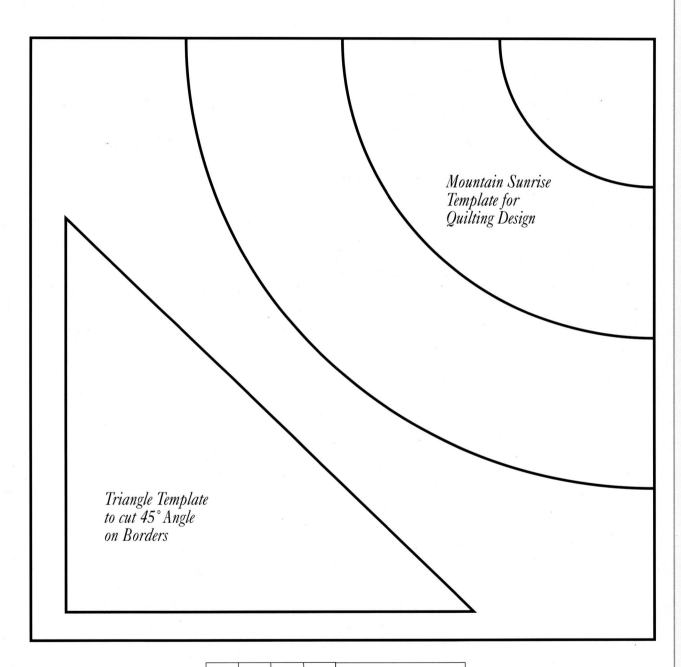

*Mountain Sunrise
Template for
Quilting Design*

*Triangle Template
to cut 45° Angle
on Borders*

Chapter Twelve
BEAR'S PAW
QUILTS

CHAPTER TWELVE

Bear's Paw Quilts

This block consists of four units joined by sashing and a center post. The first set of units is a square with a border of half-square triangles on two sides. You get into a rhythm and become more efficient as you make a batch.

The Oregon Trail was first envisioned as a quilt with a Southwest flavor. The theme print is a paisley with rich blues, turquoises, and rust with a hint of gold. When it is cut into patches, no two patches are exactly alike. This adds interest in the repeated blocks. The turquoise fabric is the accent or "sparkle" in the quilt.

In *Bloomin' Bear's Paw*, the block is bordered with the background fabric and the print before it is sashed. This makes the paw units float and almost look like flowers. I chose the larger scale, tightly packed, floral paisley fabric. When it is cut apart for the pieces, the interest is created because no two pieces are the same. I think this quilt would be great with a black background and a bright jewel tone print.

In *Bear's Patch*, I pulled many different fabrics all in earth tones, then added brighter reds and golds. It was fun creating each paw as I went along. I placed all of the cut-out paw patches on a piece of flannel on the wall and built the design before sewing. This way I could see if I was using two similar colors together, which I didn't want to do. I can envision using this quilt as a centerpiece on a table or a throw on the back of a chair.

Twilight Bear's Paw has a wonderful glow to it. By arranging the individual blocks in this setting, the light ones look like they are woven in place. Because all of the Bear's Paw motifs are black, the colored shape of the block becomes dominant. Viewing the quilt from across the room allows the points in the paw to be very visible, creating a dramatic look.

BEAR'S PAW BLOCK INSTRUCTIONS

Watch out for Bear's Paws along your easy quiltmaking path. They'll steal your heart away with their bright, glowing colors. Read through all of the general instructions before you begin these projects.

Constructing the Bear's Paw Block

The Bear's Paw is made up of four paws with claws. Each paw is divided by sashing (D) and a center post (E). Each project in this chapter contains complete cutting instructions and yardage requirements. However, if you would like to change the size of your blocks, refer to the cutting guide at the right to cut Bear's Paw blocks in three different sizes. Note that if you change the block size, you will have to adjust the amount of fabric you purchase for your project.

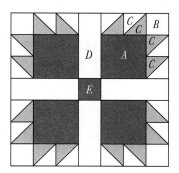

Bear's Paw Blocks

	8½"	10½"	12"
A: 4 total	3" x 3"	3½" x 3½"	3¾" x 3¾"
B: 4 total	1¾" x 1¾"	2" x 2"	2⅛" x 2⅛"
C: 8 each of claw and background	2⅛" x 2⅛"	2⅜" x 2⅜"	2½" x 2½"
D: 4 total	1½" x 4¼"	2" x 5"	2¾" x 5⅜"
E: 1 total	1½" x 1½"	2" x 2"	2¾" x 2¾"

1. Make Patch C first. Follow the cutting instructions and cut eight squares of the claw fabric and eight squares of background, then cut the squares in half diagonally. Sew the half-square triangles together, feeding pairs of fabric through the sewing machine, one after the other, without lifting the presser foot. There will be a chain of stitches between the units.

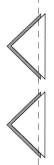

2. Clip the threads, press toward the darker fabric, and trim the excess fabric.

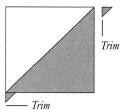

3. Arrange A, B, and C as shown. Stitch four C's together for one side, and add to A. Then stitch four C's and B together for the other side, add to A. Make a total of four.

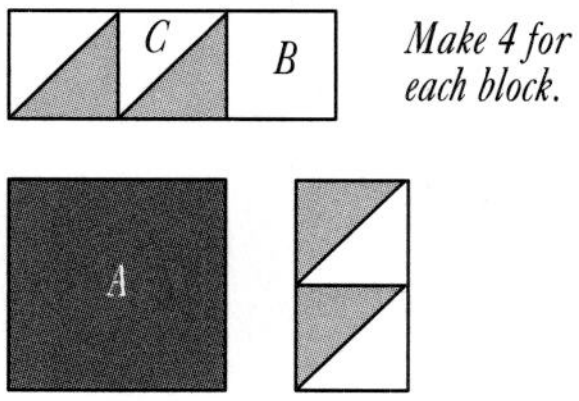

Make 4 for each block.

4. Lay out the four paws inserting sashing and the center post as shown. Stitch together in rows. Press the first and third rows toward D. Press the middle row toward D. Join the rows.

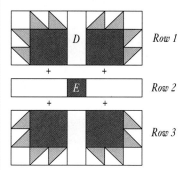

Row 1

Row 2

Row 3

THE OREGON TRAIL

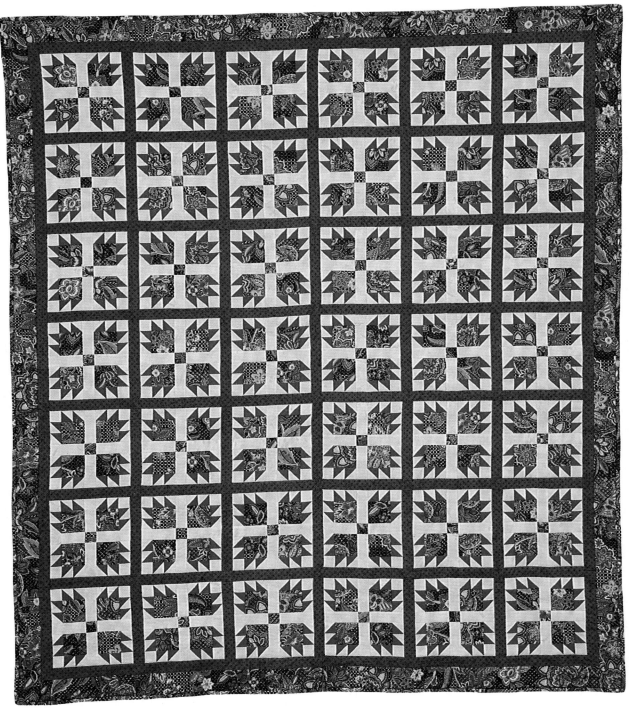

The finished size is 82" x 94". The block size is 10½".

Refer to quilt drawing and photo for color placement.

SUPPLIES

CUTTING

Paws, Second Border, and Binding
3¼ yards

Patch A: Cut 14 strips 3½" x 42". Cut into 168 squares 3½" x 3½".
Patch E: Cut two strips 2" x 42". Cut into 42 squares 2" x 2".
Border: Cut nine strips 4½" x 42" strips. Join into one long strip. From this strip cut two strips 86" for the sides; cut two strips 82" for the top and bottom.
Binding: Cut nine strips 1¾" x 42". Join into one long strip. From this strip cut two strips 94" for the sides; cut two strips 82½" for the top and bottom.

Background
2⅜ yards

Patch B: Cut eight strips 2" x 42". Cut into 168 squares 2" x 2".
Patch D: Cut 21 strips 2" x 42". Cut into 168 rectangles 2" x 5".

Claws
¾ yards

Patch C: Stack the background and claw fabrics right sides together and cut 10 strips 2⅜" x 42" of each color. Cut into 336 squares 2⅜" x 2⅜". Cut in half diagonally.

Sashing and First Border
2 yards

Vertical Sashing: Cut 12 strips 2" x 42". Cut into 35 rectangles 2" x 11".
Horizontal Sashing: Cut 11 strips 2" x 42". Join into one long strip. From this strip cut six strips 71".
First Border: Cut eight strips 2" x 42". Join into one long strip. From this strip cut two strips 83" for the sides; cut two strips 74" for the top and bottom.

Backing
5½ yards

Backing: Cut three pieces 98" x 42". Trim off the selvages and sew the sections together, right sides facing, along the lengthwise grain.

Batting 86" x 98"

SEWING INSTRUCTIONS FOR THE OREGON TRAIL

Review the Quilting Basics in Chapter 2 before you begin.

1. Follow the block directions on page 193 to make 42 blocks.

2. Arrange the blocks, inserting the vertical sashing. Sew blocks and sashing together in a row.

3. Sew horizontal sashing strips between the rows in a straight set, referring to page 33.

4. Follow the instructions on page 33 for adding the borders.

5. Follow the instructions on page 35 for basting the quilt.

6. This quilt was machine-quilted between the blocks, along the borders, and within the blocks along the sashing.

7. Follow the instructions on page 37 for binding the quilt.

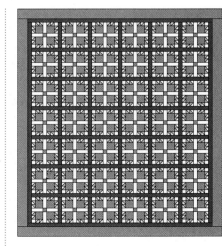

The Oregon Trail Quilt Drawing

BLOOMIN' BEAR'S PAW

The finished size is 44" x 44". The block size is 8½".

SUPPLIES

Background, First and Third Borders, Sashing, and Binding
2 yards

Floral Print for Paws, Claws, and Second Border
1⅛ yards

Backing
2⅔ yards

Batting 48" x 48"

Refer to quilt drawing and photo for color placement.

CUTTING

Patch B: Cut two strips 1¾" x 42". Cut into 36 squares 1¾" x 1¾".
Patch C: Stack the background and floral fabrics right sides together. Cut four strips 2⅛" x 42". Cut into 72 squares 2⅛" x 2⅛". Cut in half diagonally for a total of 144 triangles of each color.
Patch D: Cut four strips 1½" x 42". Cut into 36 rectangles 1½" x 4¼".
First Border around Block: Cut nine strips 1½" x 42". Open the strips and stack them. Cut two strips 9" for the sides and two strips 11" for the top and bottom of each block from each strip.
Sashing: Cut eight strips 1½" x 42". From these strips cut six strips 12" to use vertically beween the blocks and two strips 37" for the horizontal sashing.
First Border: Cut two more strips 37" for the sides, and two strips 39" for the top and bottom.
Third Border: Cut five strips 2½" x 42". From two of these, cut two strips 40" for the sides. Join the three remaining strips into one long strip. From this strip, cut two strips 44" for the top and bottom.
Binding: Cut five strips 1¾" x 42". Join into one long strip. From this strip cut two strips 44" for the sides; cut two strips 44½" for the top and bottom.

Patch A: Cut three strips 3" x 42". Cut the strips into 36 squares 3" x 3".
Patch E: Cut one strip 1½" x 15". Cut into nine squares 1½" x 1½".
Second Border around Block: Cut 12 strips 1" x 42". From these strips cut two strips 11" for the sides; cut two strips 12" for the top and bottom for each block.
Second Border: Cut four strips 1" x 42". From these strips cut two strips 39" for the sides; cut two strips 40" for the top and bottom.

Backing: Cut two pieces 48" x 42". Trim off selvages and sew pieces together, right sides facing, along the lengthwise grain.

Sewing instructions begin on next page.

SEWING INSTRUCTIONS FOR BLOOMIN' BEAR'S PAW

Review the Quilting Basics in Chapter 2 before you begin.

1. Follow the block construction directions on page 193 to make nine blocks.

2. Add the block borders as shown below.

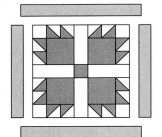

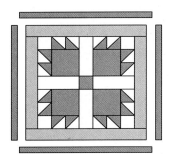

3. Lay out blocks, inserting the sashing between blocks and between rows. Follow the straight set instructions on page 33 for sewing the blocks together

Bloomin' Bear's Paw Quilt Drawing

4. Follow the instructions on page 33 for adding the borders.

5. Follow the instructions on page 35 for basting the quilt.

6. This quilt has been machine-quilted along the sashing, in the blocks, and around the borders.

7. Follow the instructions on page 37 for binding the quilt.

BEAR'S PATCH

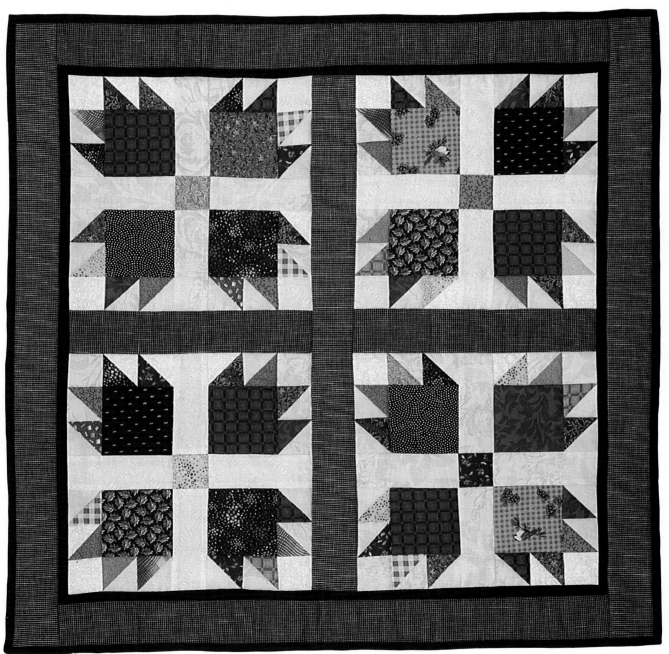

The finished size is 29" x 29". The block size is 10½".

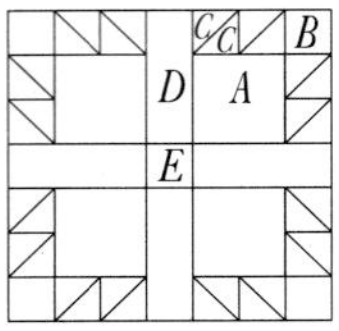

Refer to quilt drawing and photo for color placement.

SUPPLIES	CUTTING
Several Fabrics for Paw Prints 1 yard total	**Patch A:** Cut 16 squares 3½" x 3½". **Patch C:** Cut 32 squares 2⅜" x 2⅜". Cut in half diagonally. **Patch E:** Cut four squares 2" x 2".
Three Fabrics for Background 1 yard total	**Patch B:** Cut 16 squares 2" x 2". **Patch C:** Cut 32 squares 2⅜" x 2⅜". Cut in half diagonally. **Patch D:** Cut 16 rectangles 2" x 5".
Sashing and Second Border ½ yard	**Sashing:** Cut two strips 2½" x 42". Open the strips and stack them. From these strips cut two strips 11" and one strip 23½". **Second Border:** Cut three strips 2¼" x 42". Join into one long strip. From this strip cut two strips 25½" for the sides; cut two strips 29" for the top and bottom.
First Border and Binding ⅜ yard	**First Border:** Cut three strips 1½" x 42". Join into one long strip. From this strip cut two strips 23½" for the sides; cut two strips 25½" for the top and bottom. **Binding:** Cut three strips 1¾" x 44". Join into one long strip. From this strip cut two strips 29" for the sides and two strips 29½" for the top and bottom.
Backing 1 yard	**Backing:** Cut one piece 33" x 33".
Batting 33" x 33"	

SEWING INSTRUCTIONS FOR BEAR'S PATCH

Review the Quilting Basics in Chapter 2 before you begin.

1. Follow the block construction directions on page 193 to make four blocks.

2. Lay out blocks and insert 11" horizontal sashing between rows. Insert 23½" sashing between vertical rows. Follow the straight set instructions on page 33 for sewing the blocks together.

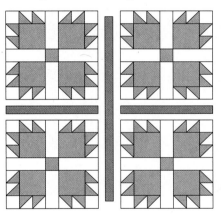

3. Follow the instructions on page 33 for adding the borders.

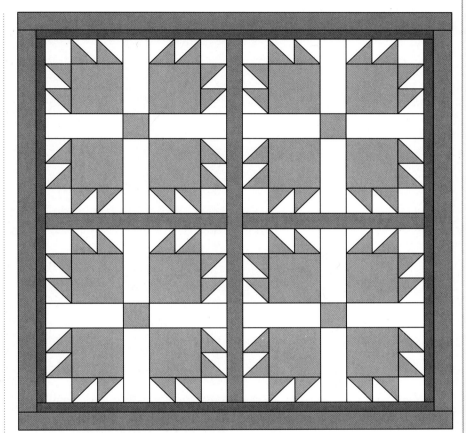

Bear's Patch Quilt Drawing

4. Follow the instructions on page 35 for basting the quilt.

5. This quilt was machine-quilted along the sashing, in the blocks, and around the borders.

6. Follow the instructions on page 37 for binding the quilt.

TWILIGHT BEAR'S PAW

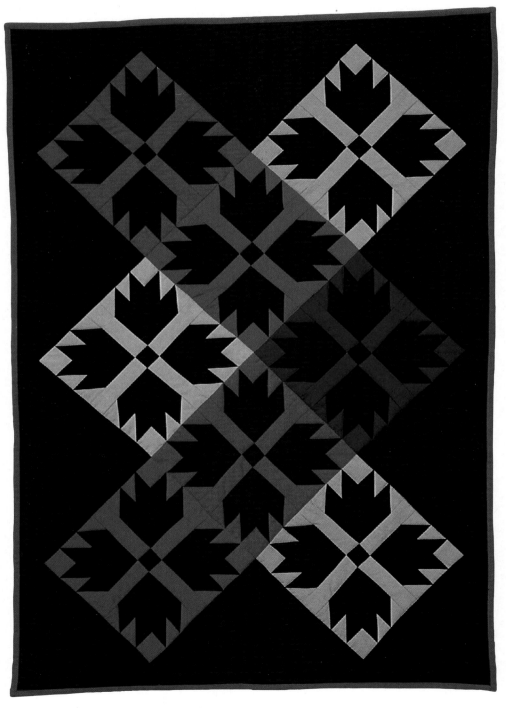

The finished size is 28" x 40". The block size is 8½".

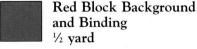

Refer to quilt drawing and photo for color placement.

SUPPLIES

Red Block Background and Binding
½ yard

Magenta, Aqua, Green and Lavender Block Backgrounds
¼ yard of four colors

Paws, Setting and Corner Triangles, and Border
1½ yards

Backing
1¼ yards

Batting 32" x 44"

CUTTING

Binding: Cut four strips 1¾" x 42". From these strips cut two strips 40" for the sides; cut two strips 28½" for the top and bottom.
Stack the red, magenta, and aqua.
Patch B: Cut one strip 1¾" x 15" of each color.
Cut into eight squares 1¾" x 1¾".
Patch C: Cut one strip 2⅛" x 42" of each color.
Cut into 16 squares 2⅛" x 2⅛". Cut in half diagonally.
Patch D: Cut one strip 1½" x 36" of each color.
Cut into eight strips 1½" x 4¼".
Stack the green and lavender.
Patch B: Cut one strip 1¾" x 8" of each color.
Cut into four squares 1¾" x 1¾" of each color.
Patch C: Cut one strip 2⅛" x 18" of each color.
Cut into eight squares 2⅛" x 2⅛". Cut in half diagonally.
Patch D: Cut one strip 1½" x 18" of each color.
Cut into four strips 1½" x 4¼".

Patch A: Cut three strips 3" x 42". Cut into 32 squares 3" x 3".
Patch C: Cut four strips 2⅛" x 42". Cut into 64 squares 2⅛" x 2⅛".
Cut in half diagonally.
Patch E: Cut one strip 1½" x 13". Cut into eight squares 1½" x 1½".
Setting Triangles: Cut two squares 13¼" x 13¼".
Cut into quarters diagonally.
Corner Triangles: Cut two squares 6⅞" x 6⅞". Cut in half diagonally.
Border: Cut four strips 2¼" x 42". From these strips cut two strips 36" for the sides; cut two strips 28" for the top and bottom.

Backing: Cut one piece 32" x 44".

SEWING INSTRUCTIONS FOR TWILIGHT BEAR'S PAW

Review the Quilting Basics in Chapter 2 before you begin.

1. Follow the directions on page 193 to make eight blocks.

2. Follow the diagonal set instructions on page 33 for sewing the blocks together.

3. Follow the instructions on page 33 for adding the borders.

4. Follow the instructions on page 35 for basting the quilt.

5. This quilt was machine-quilted along the sashing, in the blocks, and around the borders. Find a quilting design you like, draw on and quilt in the black background areas.

6. Follow the instructions on page 37 for binding the quilt.

Twilight Bear's Paw Quilt Drawing

HOUSES AND TREES QUILTS

CHAPTER THIRTEEN

Houses and Trees Quilts

I've always been fascinated by pieced pictorial quilt blocks. Houses and trees are familiar subject matter to all of us, and this is a place where you can easily insert your own style. Just look around your neighborhood for color and fabric ideas. Two simple house and three tree styles are included in various settings.

A cottage-style house appears with an apple tree in *Hood River Apple Orchard.* The large apple print plays a major role in this quilt design, appearing in the trees and the border. The gold in the doors and windows helps to add interest to the palette.

Sunflower Farm takes the apple tree shape and extends it to look like the taller poplar trees that you see by old farmhouses. In this palette, the doors and windows are black, and the roofs are plaid. The other solids in the palette switch places in the houses to create interest. The quilt reminds me of a farmhouse set in the hills of Eastern Oregon or the midwest plains.

Each of the previous quilts follows the same design format with rows of houses and trees and a strip of ground fabric. A medallion-style setting was used in *Pinebrook* with the four houses clustered in the center. The sashing had to be adjusted to accept the tree repeat in the border. Look at all of the different fabrics that have been used in the houses and trees. They all have a mood or color scheme in common, so they work together. The bright solid-blue sashing holds the design together and gives the quilt continuity.

Emily's Cottage is made of a variety of solids with the windows, doors, and chimneys as repeated fabrics. The large leafy print was the inspiration for the palette and appears as sashings and in the final border. I can see this design as a simple two- or three-color quilt such as red, black, and muslin or in blues and white. Its design feels quite traditional.

Christmas Village was a fun quilt to do. It combines two house designs and the Pine Tree block. The Milky Way Star block (see page 89) borders the quilt. Holiday reds and greens combine in the houses and trees with a bright white snowflake fabric in the background.

HOUSE AND TREE BLOCK INSTRUCTIONS

Your easy quiltmaking journey will carry you right into the Houses and Trees of this chapter.
Read through all of the general instructions before you begin these projects.

Block Construction

You will need to make templates for odd-sized pieces where indicated. Templates appear on pages 225-227. Instructions for making templates are on page 29. All House and Tree blocks are constructed in units that are joined in rows. Then the rows are stitched together. Each unit within a row must first be stitched together before one row is joined to the next.

House Block Construction

Place all of the pieces that you have cut for the House block in order next to your sewing machine. Follow the illustration below and stitch the units together in each row.

Row 1: Stitch A to B to A to B to A, and press.

Row 2: Stitch C to D to E to C, and press.

Row 3: Stitch I to J to I, and press. Add F and K, and press. Stitch G to H to G, and press. Add F. Stitch the two units together, and press.

Join Rows 1, 2 and 3 to complete the block.

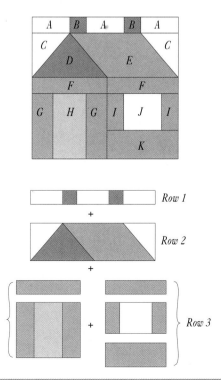

Cottage Block Construction

Row 1: Stitch A to B to A, and press.

Row 2: Stitch C to D to C, and press.

Row 3: Stitch I to H, and press. Add G to each side, and press. Make two of these, and stitch on either side of J; press. Add E, and press. Add F to each side; press. Join rows 1, 2, and 3.

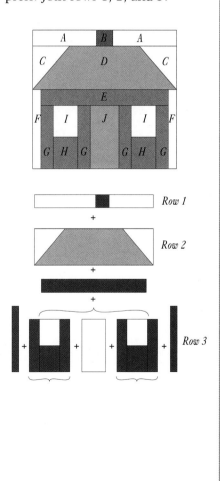

Pine Tree Block Construction

1. Place A on the left side of B and stitch from the bottom of B to the top. This will look odd when you place the two together. Lightly press seam allowances toward A without stretching the fabric.

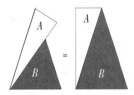

2. Add A to the right side of B, and press.

3. Add C to D to C, and press.

4. Join the two rows.

Poplar Tree Block Construction

1. Fold the four D squares in half diagonally, wrong sides together, and press. Place on the four corners of A. Stitch on the fold. Trim off excess seam allowances. Press open to the right side.

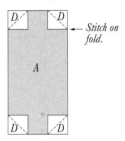

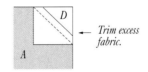

2. Stitch C to B to C, and press.

3. Join the two rows.

Apple Tree Block Construction

Section A is background fabric to appear as sky in the block.

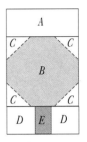

1. Fold the four C squares in half diagonally, wrong sides together, and press. Place on the four corners of B. Stitch on the fold. Trim off excess seam allowances. Press open to the right side.

2. Stitch D to E to D, and press.

3. Join the rows.

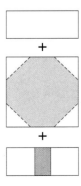

HOOD RIVER
APPLE ORCHARD

The finished size is 29" x 32".

Refer to quilt drawing and photo for color placement. Refer to figure block illustration as you cut out the Cottage and Apple Tree patches. Lay them in order beside your sewing machine. Make templates for Cottage patches C and D (page 226). All of the blocks are identical so the pieces may be stacked.

SUPPLIES

Background 1/3 yard	
Roof, First Border, and Binding 1/2 yard	
Cottages 1/4 yard	
Chimney 1½" x 7" scrap	
Doors and Windows 1/8 yard	
Apple Trees and Second Border 5/8 yard	
Tree Trunk 1½" x 11" scrap	
Ground 1/4 yard	
Backing 1 yard	
Batting 33" x 36"	

CUTTING

Cottage Background
Patch A: Cut one strip 1½" x 42". Cut into eight strips 4".
Patch C: Cut one strip 2½" x 26". Fold in half.
Use cottage template C (page 226) to cut four.
(This gives four for the left side and four for the right side.)
Patch F: Cut one strip 1" x 42". Cut into eight strips 5".
Apple Tree Background
Patch A: Cut one strip 2½" x 19". Cut into four strips 4½".
Patch C: Cut one strip 1½" x 25". Cut into 16 squares 1½" x 1½".
Patch D: Cut one strip 2" x 21". Cut into eight strips 2½".

Patch D (roof): Cut one strip 3" x 42".
Use cottage template D (page 226) to cut four.
First Border: Cut three strips 1½" x 42". Join into one long strip.
From this strip cut two strips 21½" for the sides; cut two strips 26½" for the top and bottom.
Binding: Cut four strips 1¼" x 42". From these strips cut two strips 29" for the sides; cut two strips 32½" for the top and bottom.

Cottage
Patch E: Cut one strip 1½" x 31". Cut into four strips 7½".
Patch G: Cut one strip 4" x 21". Cut into 16 strips 1¼".
Patch H: Cut one strip 1¼" x 19". Cut into eight strips 2¼".

Patch B: Cut one strip 1½" x 7". Cut into four squares 1½" x 1½".

Patch J (door): Cut one strip 2" x 17". Cut into four strips 4".
Patch I (windows): Cut one strip 1¼" x 19". Cut into eight strips 2¼".

Patch B (Apple Tree): Cut one strip 4½" x 19".
Cut into four squares 4½" x 4½".
Second Border: Cut four strips 3¼" x 42". From these strips cut two strips 23½" for the sides; cut two strips 32" for the top and bottom.

Patch E (trunk): Cut one strip 1½" x 11". Cut into four strips 2½".

Ground: Cut two strips 3" x 24½".

Backing: Cut one piece 33" x 36".

SEWING INSTRUCTIONS FOR HOOD RIVER APPLE ORCHARD

Review the Quilting Basics in Chapter 2 before you begin.

1. Make four Cottage blocks and four Apple Tree blocks following block construction directions on pages 207-208.

2. Arrange Cottage and Apple Tree blocks, and the ground as shown. Follow the straight set instructions on page 33 for sewing the blocks together.

3. Follow the instructions on page 33 for adding the borders.

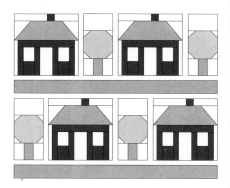

4. Follow the instructions on page 35 for basting the quilt.

5. This quilt was machine-quilted in-the-ditch.

6. Follow the instructions on page 37 for binding the quilt.

Hood River Apple Orchard Quilt Drawing

SUNFLOWER FARM

The finished size is 41" x 61½". The House block size is 8". The Poplar Tree block size is 4" x 8".

Refer to quilt drawing and photo for color placement.
Refer to block illustrations as you cut out the Houses and Poplar Trees.
Lay them in order beside your sewing machine. You may wish to stack them.
Make templates for House patches C, D, and E on page 225.

SUPPLIES

CUTTING

Background
1 yard

House Background
Patch A: Cut a strip 2½" x 42". Cut into 27 rectangles 2½" x 1½".
Patch C: Cut two strips 3" x 42". Place right sides together,
and cut out nine patches using House template C (page 225).
This gives nine left and nine right background pieces.
Poplar Tree Background
Patch D: Cut two strips 1½" x 42". Cut into 48 squares 1½" each.
Patch C: Cut one strip 2" x 42" and one strip 2" x 21";
cut into 24 rectangles 2" x 2½".
Side Panels: Cut six 2" x 42" strips. Cut into 24 strips 2" x 8½".

Roof
¼ yard

Patch E (roof): Cut a strip 7" x 28".
Using House template E (page 225) cut out nine roofs.

Door, Window,
Chimney, First Border,
and Binding
¾ yard

Patch H (door): Cut one strip 2" x 42". Cut into nine rectangles 2" x 4".
Patch J (window): Cut one strip 2½" x 24". Cut into nine squares 2½" x 2½".
Patch B (chimney): Cut one strip 1½" x 28". Cut into 18 squares 1½" x 1½".
First Border: Cut four strips 1½" x 42". Join in one long strip. From this strip
cut two strips 32" for the sides; cut two strips 54½" for the top and bottom.
Binding: Cut five strips 1¾" x 42". Join in one long strip. From this strip
cut two strips 41" for the side; cut two strips 62" for the top and bottom.

Houses
¾ yard total from
variety of fabrics

Houses: *(You may wish to change colors in each house . If so, cut out pieces
for two or three houses at a time by stacking the fabric.) Total needed for all
houses will be given in ( ) but the cutting instructions are for a single house.*
Patch D: Cut one rectangle using House template D (page 225)(9).
Patch F (house side): Cut one rectangle 1½" x 4½ " (9).
Patch F (house front): Cut one rectangle 1½" x 4½" (9).
Patch G: Cut two rectangles 1¾" x 4" (18).
Patch I: Cut two rectangles 1½" x 2½" (18).
Patch K: Cut one rectangle 2" x 4½" (9).

Poplar Tree and
Second Border
1 yard

Patch A (tree): Cut two strips 4½" x 42". Cut into 12 rectangles 4½" x 6½".
Second Border: Cut five strips 4" x 42". Join in one long strip.
From this strip cut two strips 34" for the sides; cut two strips 61½" for
the top and bottom.

Trunk
1½" x 31"
⅛ yard

Patch B (trunk): Cut a strip 1½" x 31". Cut into 12 rectangles 1½" x 2½".

Ground
⅜ yard

Ground: Cut four strips 3" x 42". Join in one long strip.
From this strip cut three strips 52½".

Backing
2½ yards

Backing: Cut two pieces 42" x 45". Trim off the selvages, and sew sections
together, right sides facing, along the lengthwise grain (45" sides).

Batting 45" x 66"

Sewing instructions begin on next page.

SEWING INSTRUCTIONS FOR SUNFLOWER FARM

Review the Quilting Basics in Chapter 2 before you begin.

1. Make nine House and twelve Poplar Tree blocks following block construction directions on pages 207-208.

2. Arrange House and Poplar Tree blocks in rows inserting side panels on each side of the tree. Follow the straight set instructions on page 33 for sewing the blocks together.

3. Follow the instructions on page 33 for adding the borders.

4. Follow the instructions on page 35 for basting the quilt.

5. This quilt was machine-quilted in-the-ditch.

6. Follow the instructions on page 37 for binding the quilt.

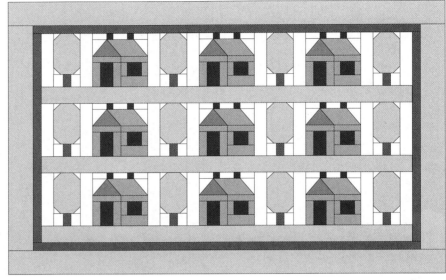

Sunflower Farm Quilt Drawing

PINEBROOK

The finished size is 36½" x 36½". The House block size is 8". The Pine Tree block size is 4" x 8".

Refer to quilt drawing and photo for color placement. Refer to block illustrations as you cut out the House and Pine Tree patches. Lay in order beside your sewing machine. Make templates for Pine Tree patches A and B and House patches C, D, and E on pages 225 and 227.
Note: This house has only one chimney.

SUPPLIES

Background
1⅛ yard

Chimney,
Door, Window
¼ yard

Houses, Roofs
1½ yards total of a
variety of fabrics

Pine Trees
scraps to total
½ yard

Tree Trunks and
Binding
⅜ yard

Sashing and
Border
¼ yard

Backing
1⅛ yard

Batting 41" x 41"

CUTTING

House Background
Patch A: Cut two strips 1½" x 42".
Cut into eight rectangles 1½" x 2½" and eight rectangles 1½" x 5½".
Patch C: Cut one strip 3" x 42". Fold in half.
Cut eight using House template C (page 225).
This gives eight for the left side and eight for the right side.
Pine Tree Background
Patch A: Cut three strips 7½" x 42". Fold in half lengthwise.
Cut 20 using Pine Tree template A (page 227).
This will give you 20 for the left side and 20 for the right side.
Patch C: Cut two strips 2" x 42". Cut into 40 squares 2" x 2".

Patch B (chimney): Cut one strip 1½" x 13". Cut into eight squares 1½" x 1½".
Patch H (door): Cut one strip 2" x 33". Cut into eight rectangles 2" x 4".
Patch J (window): Cut one strip 2½" x 21". Cut into eight squares 2½" x 2½".

The roof and house parts are all different fabrics. The dimensions for cutting the piece will be given and the total number needed in ( ).
Stack the fabrics to facilitate cutting.
Patch D: Cut one using House template D (page 225)(8).
Patch E (roof): Cut one using House template E (page 225)(8).
Patch F (House Side): Cut one rectangle 1½" x 4½" (8).
Patch F (House Front): Cut one rectangle 1½" x 4½" (8).
Patch G: Cut two rectangles 1¾" x 4" (16).
Patch I: Cut two rectangles 1½" x 2½" (16).
Patch K: Cut one rectangle 2" x 4½" (8).

The trees are all different fabrics. Stack the fabrics for ease in cutting.
Patch B (tree): Use Pine Tree template B (page 227) to cut 20 trees.

Patch D (trunk): Cut one strip 2" x 31". Cut into 20 rectangles 2" x 1½".
Binding: Cut four strips 1¾" x 42". From these strips cut two strips 36½" for the sides; cut two strips 37" for the top and bottom.

Sashing: Cut one strip 2" x 42". Open the strip.
From this strip cut two strips 2" x 8½"; cut one strip 2" x 18".
Border: Cut two strips 1¾" x 42". Open the strips.
From one strip, cut two strips 18" for the sides.
From the other strip, cut two strips 20½" for the top and bottom.

Backing: Cut one piece 41" x 41".

SEWING INSTRUCTIONS FOR PINEBROOK

Review the Quilting Basics in Chapter 2 before you begin.

1. Make eight House blocks and 20 Pine Tree blocks following the block construction directions on pages 207-208.

2. Place the sashing between the four center blocks as shown. Follow the straight set instructions on page 33 for sewing the blocks together.

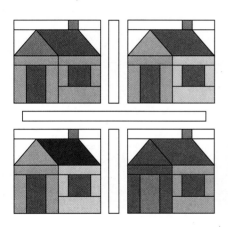

3. Follow the instructions on page 33 for adding the first border.

4. Following the figure to the right, stitch House and Pine Tree borders together and add to the center of the quilt.

Pinebrook Quilt Drawing

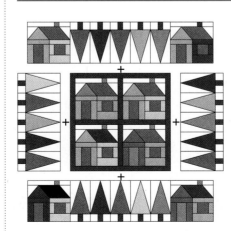

5. Follow the instructions on page 35 for basting the quilt.

6. This quilt was stitched in-the-ditch between the blocks.

7. Follow the instructions on page 37 for binding the quilt.

EMILY'S COTTAGE

The finished size is 29½" x 38½". The block size is 8".

CHRISTMAS VILLAGE

The finished size is 59" x 59". The House and Cottage block sizes are 8". The Pine Tree block is 4" x 8".

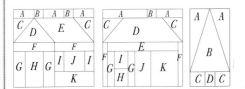

Refer to quilt drawing and photo for color placement.
Refer to block illustrations as you cut out the houses and trees.
Lay them in order beside your sewing machine.

SUPPLIES

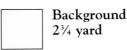

Background
2¾ yard

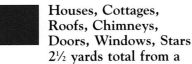

Houses, Cottages,
Roofs, Chimneys,
Doors, Windows, Stars
2½ yards total from a
variety of fabrics

CUTTING

Backgrounds: *Make template C for the houses (page 225), template C for the cottages (page 226), and template A for the pine trees (page 227). See Milky Way Stars in section below for background patch B cut with sky fabric.*

For Houses
Patch A: Cut two strips 1½" x 42". Cut into 30 rectangles 1½" x 2½".
Patch C: Cut two strips 3" x 42". Place right sides together and cut out 20 using House template C. (This gives 10 for the left side and 10 for the right side.)
Background Spacers Between Houses: Cut one strip 8½" x 42".
Cut into eight rectangles 8½" x 1½" and six rectangles 8½" x 2½".

For Cottages
Patch A: Cut two strips 1½" x 42". Cut nine rectangles 1½" x 4½" and nine rectangles 1½" x 3½".
Patch C: Cut one strip 3¼" x 42". Fold strip in half.
Use Cottage template C (page 226) to cut nine. (This gives nine for the left and nine for the right side of the house.)
Patch F: Cut one strip 5" x 19". Cut into 18 rectangles 5" x 1".

For Pine Trees
Patch A: Cut three strips 7½" x 42". Fold in half lengthwise.
Using Pine Tree template A (page 227), cut 34. (This will give you 17 for the left and 17 for the right side.)
Patch C: Cut two strips 2" x 42". Cut into 34 squares 2" x 2".

For Milky Way Stars
Patch A: Cut nine strips 2" x 42" and one strip 2" x 7".
Cut into 192 squares 2" x 2".

Houses: *Make templates for D and E for the houses (page 225).*
Total pieces needed for all houses will be given in ( ) but most cutting instructions will be for a single house. Ten houses are required.
Patch B (chimney): Cut one square 1½" x 1½" (20).
Patch D: Cut one from template D (10).
Patch E (roof): Cut one from template E (10).
Patch F (House Side): Cut one rectangle 1½" x 4½" (10).
Patch F (House Front): Cut one rectangle 1½" x 4½" (10).
Patch G: Cut two rectangles 1¾" x 4" (20).
Patch H (door): Cut one rectangle 2" x 4" (10).
Patch I: Cut two rectangles 1½" x 2½" (20).
Patch J (window): Cut one square 2½" x 2½" (10).
Patch K: Cut one rectangle 2" x 4½" (10).

SUPPLIES

CUTTING

Cottages: Make template D for the cottages. Notice that there is only a window on one side of the door, and the chimney is offset to the right. K replaces the window unit. Nine cottages are required.
Patch D (roof): Cut one from Cottage template D (page 226)(9).
Patch B (chimney): Cut one square 1½" x 1½" (9).
Patch E: Cut one rectangle 1½" x 7½" (9).
Patch G: Cut two rectangles 1¼" x 4" (18).
Patch H: Cut one rectangle 1¾" x 2¼" (9).
Patch K: Cut one rectangle 3¼" x 4" (9).
Patch I (window): Cut one rectangle 1¼" x 2¼" (9).
Milky Way Stars
Patch B: From star and background fabrics, cut six strips 2⅜" x 42". Place a background and star fabric facing each other and stack three pairs of these on top of each other to facilitate cutting. Cut 96 squares 2⅜" x 2⅜". Cut in half diagonally. (Or use the grid method discussed on page 28 for making half-square triangles.)
Patch C: Cut two strips 2" x 42" and one strip 2" x 13". Cut into 48 squares 2" x 2".

	Pine Trees ¾ yard total from a variety of fabrics	**Patch B (tree):** Use Pine Tree template B (page 227) to cut 17. **Patch D (tree trunk):** Cut one strip 1½" x 34". Cut into 17 rectangles 1½" x 2".
	Tree Trunks ⅛ yard	
	Ground ⅜ yard	**Ground:** Cut five strips 2½" x 42". Join into one long strip. From this strip cut into four strips 48½".
	First Border, **Binding** ⅝ yard	**First Border:** Cut five strips 1¼" x 42". Join into one long strip. From this strip cut two strips 48½" for the sides; cut two strips 50" for the top and bottom. **Binding:** Cut six strips 1¾" x 42". Join into one long strip. From this strip cut two strips 59" for the sides; cut two strips 59½" for the top and bottom.
	Backing 3½ yards	**Backing:** Cut two pieces 42" x 63". Trim off the selvages and sew sections together, right sides facing, along the lengthwise grain.
	Batting 63" x 63"	

Sewing instructions begin on next page.

SEWING INSTRUCTIONS FOR CHRISTMAS VILLAGE

Review the Quilting Basics in Chapter 2 before you begin.

1. Make 10 House blocks, nine Cottage blocks, and 17 Pine Tree blocks following the block construction directions on pages 207-208.

2. Make 48 Milky Way Star blocks. Refer to the instructions on page 89.

3. Follow the drawing below and place the blocks in rows. There are background spacers of two different widths in the rows. Follow the straight set instructions on page 33 for sewing the blocks together.

4. Sew row 1 to the ground strip, then add row 2, and so forth.

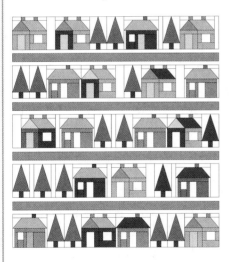

5. Follow the instructions on page 33 for adding the first border.

6. Arrange the Milky Way Stars in two rows of 11 and add to the sides of the quilt as you would a border. Make two rows of 13 and add to the top and bottom.

Christmas Village Quilt Drawing

7. Follow the instructions on page 35 for basting the quilt.

8. This quilt was machine-quilted in-the-ditch between the blocks.

9. Follow instructions on page 37 for binding the quilt.

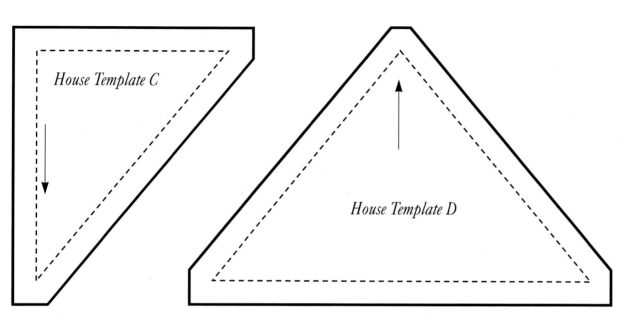

House Template C

House Template D

Arrows indicate grain line.

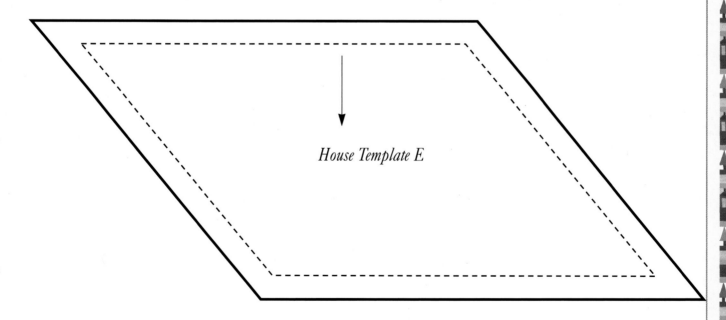

House Template E

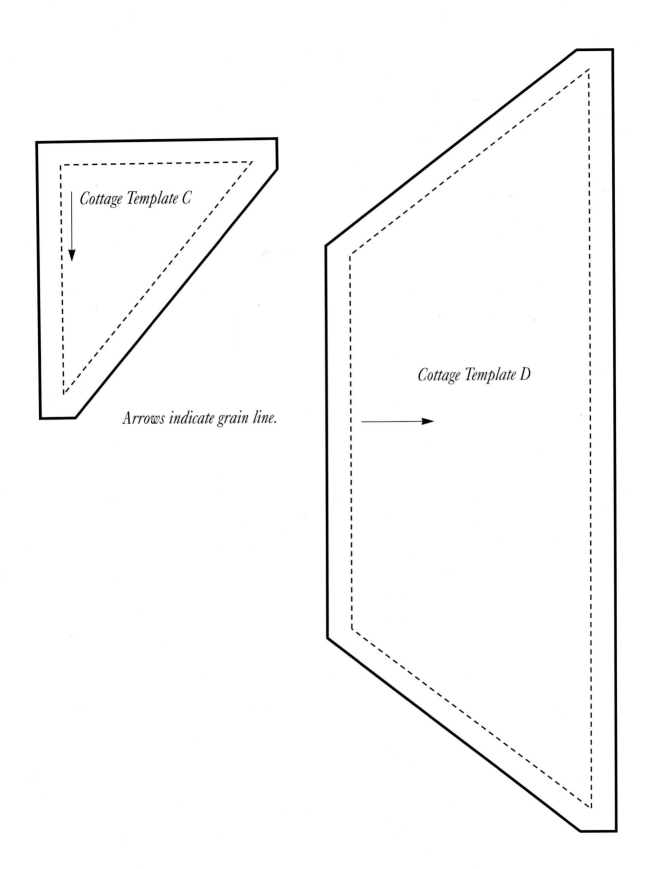

Cottage Template C

Arrows indicate grain line.

Cottage Template D

Arrows indicate grain line.

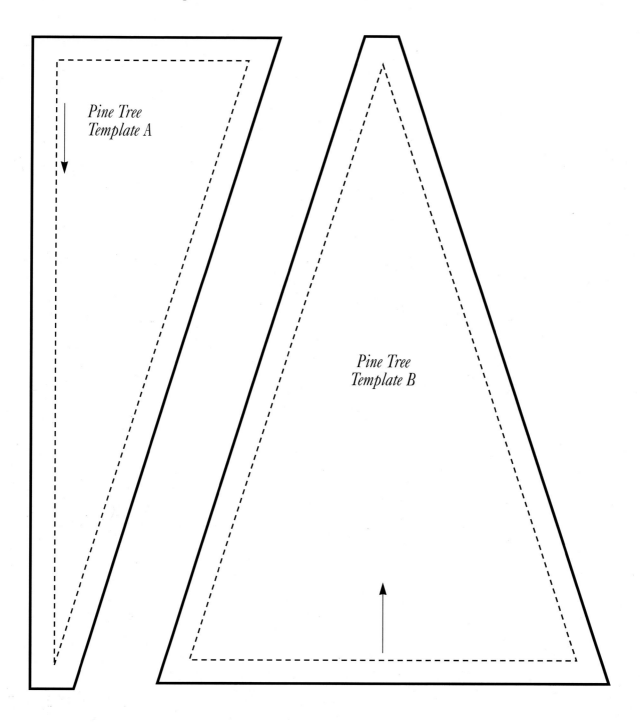

*Pine Tree
Template A*

*Pine Tree
Template B*

Chapter Fourteen
SAMPLER QUILTS

CHAPTER FOURTEEN

Sampler Quilts

Sampler classes are my very favorite to teach at my store. They teach a variety of techniques in one single quilt. You also learn how to compose a quilt setting. I try to make my classes comprehensive and squeeze in as much basic information about quilting as I can. I have started my 10th sampler, and I can still think of more to make.

These sampler quilts are composed of the various blocks in this book. (You may wish to refer to the sewing instructions in the individual chapters.) You will see these blocks in a new light. Each block needs to be treated as a separate composition as you make it. Always look for things to repeat throughout the quilt like color combinations, or settings. This will give the quilt design continuity. I always tell my students that they have met the test when they start saying "My quilt *needs* this or that"—instead of saying "I want this or that." Learning to please the quilt is my ultimate goal for students in quilt design.

It is helpful to put flannel or dense batting on a wall, if only for a short time. Your blocks will stick to the flannel, and you can observe them from a distance. The colors and design are put in perspective when you do this. In one of the quilts I was making, I was always using a version of tan for the background in each block. I really liked my Bear's Paw block, but at the end of class, when I saw it from a distance with the others, it stuck out like a sore thumb because the background was so much lighter than the other blocks. I had only used it once. So it found a place on the back of the quilt instead of the front.

In this chapter, I have included some simple wall quilts and a larger version containing 12 blocks. Each quilt has a different composition to give you even more ideas. Most of the time, I find a theme fabric to help me in selecting the other companions. Then I always need an accent— something a little more contrasty that makes the others work together.

The *Garden Sampler* was the first one I made, and I love its sunny disposition. I had been itching to use sunflower fabric in something ever since it came on the market. The fabric choices are simple: three yellows, two greens, two flowers, two black-and-whites. The ¼" stripe used in the House block and in the border makes the quilt sing. Even though the yellow is bright and cheery, the stripe was needed. Sometimes, a different style of fabric like a stripe used with florals will improve the design. I felt this particular stripe resembled a fence, which fit in with the garden theme.

This four block sampler is a great launching pad for the beginning quilter. You get a variety of piecing experiences in the four blocks plus the appliquéd hearts. Some other ideas for color combinations might be all intense brights using the blacks where I have, or try red, white, and blue using a star fabric for the theme. It would be very pretty in pastels with a lot of white.

Gone Fishing is a small wall quilt that you might see hanging in a den, an entry way, or a fishing cabin. Fish fabric was used for the theme. You will see pieces of it used as blocks. The blocks are set in horizontal rows with strips separating the units. The scale of the blocks was kept smaller for this intimate style of quilt. It's fun to find ways to use unusual fabric within the block setting.

Since *Gone Fishing* is a smaller quilt, it will fit in a smaller space or could become part of a grouping on a wall. You will need to choose fabrics that have a variety of scales in them. A large print will not work as well because the pieces are smaller. A medium size print coupled with a variety of smaller prints in different styles will be most interesting.

Donna's Sampler is dedicated to my long-time friend Donna Wilder, marketing vice president for Fairfield Processing. For my birthday, Donna designed a quilt using the 4" swatches from Fabric Finders, the fabric club at my store. She used the setting shown on page 238 with the muslin surrounded by a black-and-white print for the sashing and border. With sashing like this, you can use a wide variety of colors and fabrics in the blocks. If you look closely at this quilt, you'll see there is a little bit of everything in it. There are blocks that are warm and inviting, blocks that are cool and icy, ones that have a pastel Victorian look.

The key to the design is that you concentrate on the fabrics in each block as a separate entity while you plan it, but all of these separate entities work well in this setting. Make sure the fabrics coordinate with each other within the block. Then the sashing will take care of holding the variety of blocks together. The choice of neutrals—the muslin and the small black-and-white print—for the sashing borders is a separate color palette creating unity in the design. This is truly a scrap quilt, one that you can do with little bits and leftover pieces.

GARDEN SAMPLER

The finished size is 37¾" x 37¾". The block size is 12".

Refer to quilt drawing and photo for color placement.
You will need to make templates for some patches.

SUPPLIES	CUTTING

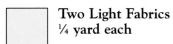 **Sunflower Theme Print for Third Border and Patchwork**
¼ yard

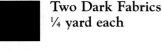 **Two Light Fabrics**
¼ yard each

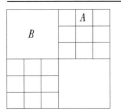 **Two Dark Fabrics**
¼ yard each

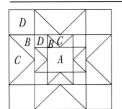 **Four Medium Fabrics**
¼ yard each

Third Border: Cut four strips 3½" x 42".
From these strips cut two strips 31¾" for the sides;
cut two strips 37¾" for the top and bottom.

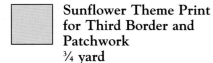

Nine Patch
Patch A: Cut 18 squares 2½" x 2½" from various fabrics.
Patch B: Cut two squares 6½" x 6½" from theme fabric.

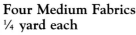

Milky Way
Patch A: Cut eight squares 2½" x 2½" from each of two
different fabrics (16 total).
Patch B: Cut two squares 4⅞" x 4⅞" each from theme and
a light fabric (four total). Cut in half diagonally.
Patch C (Pinwheel): Cut one square 2⅞" x 2⅞" of two different fabrics.
Cut two squares 2⅞" x 2⅞" from a third fabric. Cut in half diagonally.

Sawtooth Star
• *6" Star for center:*
Patch A: Cut one square 3½" x 3½" from theme fabric.
Patch B: Cut eight squares 2" x 2" from theme fabric.
Patch C: Cut four rectangles 2" x 3½" from dark fabric.
Patch D: Cut four squares 2" x 2" from same dark fabric.
• *12" Star:*
Patch A: Use 6" Star (made above).
Patch B: Using the same dark fabric as you used for C and D in the
6" star, cut eight squares 3½" x 3½".
Patch C: Cut four rectangles 3½" x 6½" from light fabric.
Patch D: Cut four squares 3½" x 3½" from same light fabric as Patch C.

Chart continues on next page.

SUPPLIES

CUTTING

House
Patch A: Cut three rectangles 1½" x 2½" from medium fabric for background.
Patch B: Cut two squares 1½" x 1½" from dark fabric for chimney.
Patch C: Cut two using template C (page 237), reversing one, from medium fabric for background.
Patch D: Cut one using template D (page 237) from theme fabric for house peak.
Patch E: Cut one using template E (page 237) from medium fabric for roof.
Patch F: Cut two rectangles 1½" x 4½" from two different medium fabrics for house side and house front.
Patch G: Cut two rectangles 1¾" x 4" from medium fabric for house front.
Patch H: Cut one rectangle 2" x 4" from dark fabric for door.
Patch I: Cut two rectangles 1½" x 2½" from theme fabric for house side.
Patch J: Cut one square 2½" x 2½" from light fabric for window.
Patch K: Cut one rectangle 2" x 4½" from theme fabric for house side.
Pine Tree
Patch A: Cut two using template A (page 236), reversing one, from medium fabric for background.
Patch B: Cut one using template B (page 236) from medium fabric for tree.
Patch C: Cut two squares 2" x 2" from medium fabric for background.
Patch D: Cut one rectangle 1½" x 2" from dark fabric for tree trunk.
Ground: Cut one strip 3½" x 12½" from same fabric as Patch B.

Sashing, First Border and Binding
⅝ yard

Sashing and First Border: Cut five strips 2¼" x 42". Open strips.
Stack two of the strips and cut from each one strip 12½" and one strip 26¼".
Stack two more strips and cut them 29¾". Cut the one remaining strip 26¼".
Binding: Cut four strips 1¾" x 42". From these strips cut two strips 37¾" for the sides; cut two strips 38¼" for the top and bottom.

Striped Fabric for Second Border and Fence
¼ yard

Second Border: Cut four strips 1½" x 42". Cut two strips 29¾" for the sides; cut two strips 31¼" for the top and bottom.
Fence: Cut one strip 1½ " x 12½" (with vertical lines) for House block.

Backing
1¼ yards

Backing: Cut one piece 42" x 42".

Batting 42" x 42"

SEWING INSTRUCTIONS FOR GARDEN SAMPLER

Review the Quilting Basics in Chapter 2 before you begin.

Instructions are given for individual blocks followed by the quilt assembly. You may need to review the construction techniques in individual chapters for each block as you go along.

Nine Patch

1. Construct two Nine Patch blocks following the instructions on page 41.

2. Stitch the 6½" square to a Nine Patch for row 1 and row 2. Join the rows.

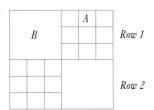

Milky Way

1. Construct the Pinwheel block that sits in the middle of the star following the instructions on page 57.

2. Follow the instructions on page 89 for assembling the Milky Way block.

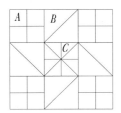

Garden Sampler Quilt Drawing

Sawtooth Star

1. Construct a 6" Star following the instructions on pages 73-74.

2. Using the 6" Star for the center, construct a 12" Star block.

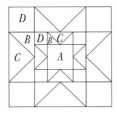

House and Pine Tree

1. Construct a House and Pine Tree following the instructions on pages 207-208. Stitch the House and Pine Tree blocks together.

2. Add the fence and ground borders at the bottom of the House.

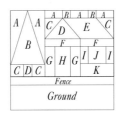

Quilt Assembly

1. Follow quilt drawing and arrange the blocks with sashing in between. Follow the straight set instructions on page 33 for sewing the blocks together.

2. Follow the instructions on page 33 for adding the borders.

3. Follow the instructions on page 35 for basting the quilt.

4. This quilt was machine-quilted in-the-ditch.

5. Follow the instructions on page 37 for binding the quilt.

Arrows indicate grain line.

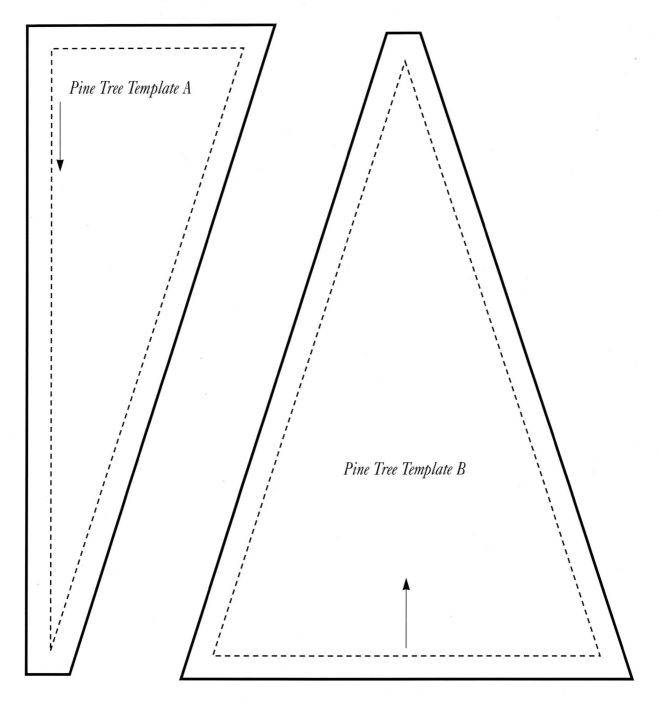

Pine Tree Template A

Pine Tree Template B

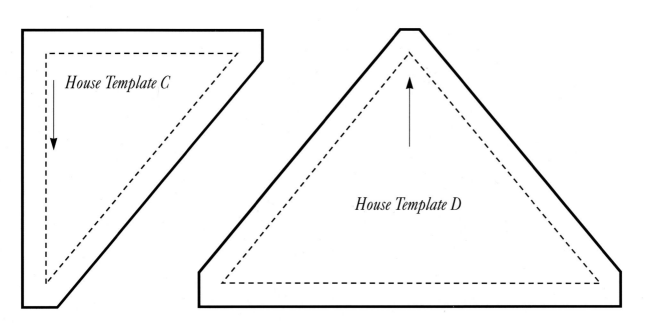

House Template C

House Template D

Arrows indicate grain line.

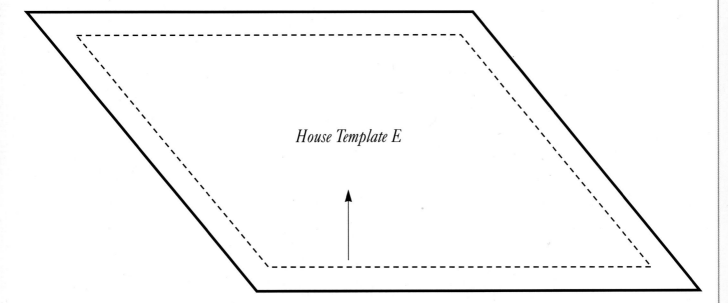

House Template E

DONNA'S SAMPLER

The finished size is 50" x 64½". The block size is 12".

Refer to quilt drawing and photo for color placement.

SUPPLIES

CUTTING

Each block has a palette of colors all its own. You will want to have lights, mediums, and darks to give contrast. None of the blocks contain over ⅓ yard total yardage. You can work from scraps that you have or with fat quarters or ⅛ yard cuts. Individual yardage is not given. You will need to make templates for some patches.

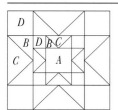

Sawtooth Star
6" Star (center)
Patch A: Cut one square 3½" x 3½" for center.
Patch B: Cut eight squares 2" x 2" for star points.
Patch C: Cut four rectangles 2" x 3½" for background.
Patch D: Cut four squares 2" x 2" for background.
12" Star
Patch A: Use 6" Star (made above).
Patch B: Using the same fabric as you used for C and D in the 6" star, cut eight squares 3½" x 3½" for star points.
Patch C: Cut four rectangles 3½" x 6½" for background.
Patch D: Cut four squares 3½" x 3½" for background.

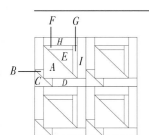

Baskets *(Cutting directions are for one basket. Make four.)*
Patch A: Cut one square 4⅞" x 4⅞". Cut in half diagonally for basket.
Patch B: Cut one square 1⅞" x 1⅞". Cut in half diagonally for basket base.
Patch C: Cut one square 2⅞" x 2⅞". Cut in half diagonally for background.
Patch D: Cut two rectangles 1½" x 4½" for background.
Patch E: Cut one square 3⅞" x 3⅞". Cut in half diagonally for background.
Patch F: Cut one rectangle 1" x 4¾" for basket handle.
Patch G: Cut one rectangle 1" x 5½" for basket handle.
Patch H: Cut one rectangle 1½" x 4½" for background.
Patch I: Cut one rectangle 1½" x 5½" for background.

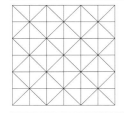

Pinwheels (9)
Cut 18 light and 18 dark squares 2⅞" x 2⅞". Cut in half diagonally.

Chart continues on next page.

SUPPLIES

CUTTING

Cottage
Patch A: Cut two rectangles 1½" x 4" for sky.
Patch B: Cut one square 1½" x 1½" for chimney.
Patch C: Cut two using Cottage template C (page 246),
reversing one, for sky.
Patch D: Cut one using Cottage template D (page 246) for roof.
Patch E: Cut one rectangle 1½" x 7½" for cottage.
Patch F: Cut two rectangles 1" x 5" for sky.
Patch G: Cut four rectangles 1¼" x 4" for cottage.
Patch H: Cut two rectangles 1¾" x 2¼" for cottage.
Patch I: Cut two rectangles 1¾" x 2¼" for windows.
Patch J: Cut one rectangle 2" x 4" for door.

Apple Tree
Patch A: Cut one rectangle 2½" x 4½" for sky.
Patch B: Cut one square 4½" x 4½" for tree.
Patch C: Cut four squares 1½" x 1½" for sky.
Patch D: Cut two rectangles 2" x 2½" for sky.
Patch E: Cut one rectangle 1½" x 2½" for trunk.
Sky: Cut one rectangle 1½" x 12½".
Ground: Cut one rectangle 3½" x 12½".

Bear's Paw
Patch A: Cut four squares 3¾" x 3¾" for paws.
Patch B: Cut four squares 2⅛" x 2⅛" for background.
Patch C: Cut eight squares 2½" x 2½" each of background
and claw fabric. Cut in half diagonally.
Patch D: Cut four rectangles 2¾" x 5⅜" for sashing.
Patch E: Cut one square 2¾" x 2¾" for center post.

Spools (4)
Patch A: Using spool template A (page 248), cut eight of each
from background and spool fabric.
Patch B: Cut four squares 2½" x 2½" for centers.

Nine Patch and Hearts
Patch A: Cut 10 squares 2½" x 2½" from one fabric and 8 more
from another fabric for Nine Patches.
Patch B: Cut two squares 6½" x 6½" for heart background.
Patch C: Using the Large Heart template (page 248), cut two hearts
from paper-backed adhesive. Fuse to wrong side of heart fabric.
Cut out and fuse to Patch B (see page 32).

SUPPLIES

CUTTING

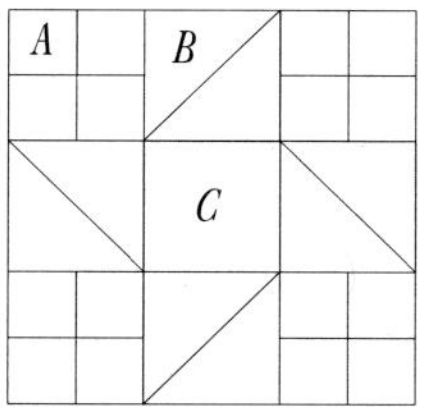

Milky Way
Patch A: Cut eight squares 2½" x 2½" from each of
two different fabrics for Four Patches.
Patch B: Cut two squares 4⅞" x 4⅞" from each of two different
fabrics for star points and background. Cut in half diagonally.
Patch C: Cut one square 4½" x 4½" for center.

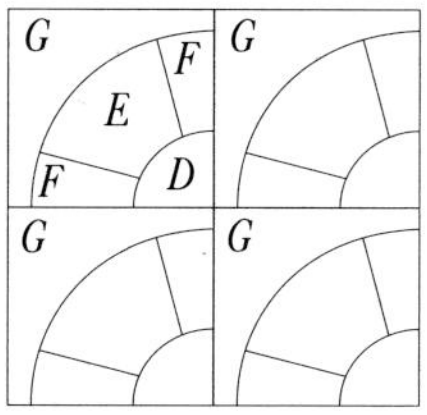

6" Fans (4)
Patch E: Cut four using Fan template E (page 247) for 6" Fan.
Patch F: Cut eight using Fan template F (page 246) for 6" Fan.
Patch D: Cut four using Fan template D (page 247) for 6" Fan base.
Patch G: Cut four using Fan template G (page 247) for background.

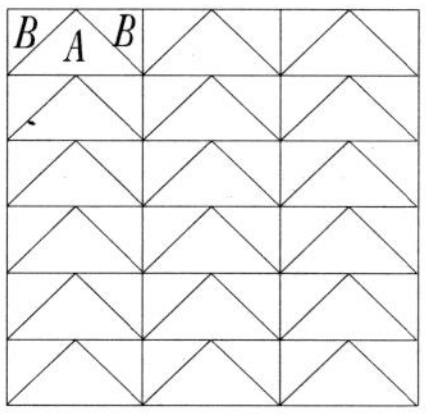

Flying Geese (18)
Patch A: Cut 18 rectangles 2½" x 4½" for geese.
Patch B: Cut 36 squares 2½" x 2½" for background.

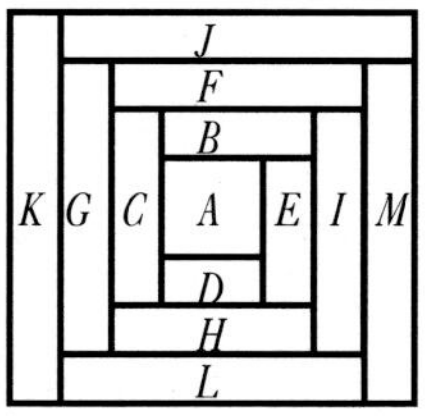

Log Cabin (4)
Patch A (center): Cut four squares 2" x 2".
Logs: All are cut 1¼" wide, lengths are given. Cut four of each.

Light Side	Dark Side
Patch B: 2"	**Patch D:** 2¾"
Patch C: 2¾"	**Patch E:** 3½"
Patch F: 3½"	**Patch H:** 4¼"
Patch G: 4¼"	**Patch I:** 5"
Patch J: 5"	**Patch L:** 5¾"
Patch K: 5¾"	**Patch M:** 6½"

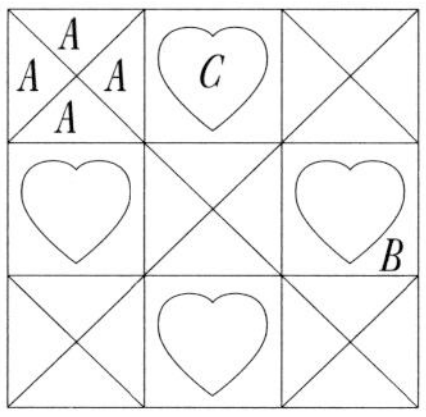

Stars and Hearts (5 pieced blocks, 4 Heart blocks)
Patch A: Cut five squares 5¼" x 5¼" from various fabrics.
Cut into quarters diagonally for pieced blocks.
Patch B: Cut four squares 4½" x 4½" for heart background.
Patch C: Using the Small Heart template (page 248),
cut four hearts from paper-backed adhesive. Fuse to wrong side
of heart fabric, cut out and fuse to patch B.
Corner Posts: Cut 20 squares 3⅜" x 3⅜" from various fabrics.
Cut in half diagonally.

Chart continues on next page.

SUPPLIES

**Muslin Sashing
and Border**
1⅛ yards

**Print Sashing
and Binding**
1⅛ yards

Backing
3 yards

Batting 54" x 69"

**Paper-backed
Adhesive for Appliqué**
⅓ yard

CUTTING

Sashing and Border: Cut 16½ strips 2" x 42" from muslin.
Cut 10½ of the strips into 31 rectangles 2" x 12½". Join the remaining six strips into one long strip. From this strip cut two strips 61" for the sides; cut two strips 49½" for the top and bottom.

Sashing: Cut 19 strips 1" x 42" from the print fabric.
Cut 21 of the strips into 62 rectangles 1" x 12½".
Binding: Cut six strips 1¾" x 42" from the print fabric.
Join into one long strip. From this strip cut two strips 65" for the sides; cut two strips 51" for the top and bottom.

Backing: Cut two pieces 42" x 54". Trim off the selvages and sew sections together, right sides facing, along the lengthwise grain.

Sewing instructions begin on page 244.

Donna's Sampler Quilt Drawing

SEWING INSTRUCTIONS FOR DONNA'S SAMPLER

Review the Quilting Basics in Chapter 2 before you begin.

Instructions are given for individual blocks followed by quilt assembly. You may need to review the construction techniques in individual chapters for each block as you go along.

Sawtooth Star

1. Construct a 6" Star following the instructions on page 73.

2. Using the 6" Star for the center, construct a 12" Star block.

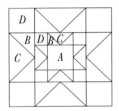

Baskets

1. Construct four Baskets following the instructions on page 157.

2. Stitch Baskets together into rows. Join rows.

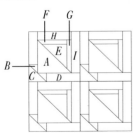

Pinwheels

1. Construct nine Pinwheels following the instructions on page 57.

2. Stitch Pinwheels together in three rows of three blocks each. Join rows.

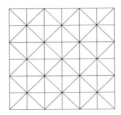

Cottage and Apple Tree

1. Construct the Cottage and Apple Tree blocks following the instructions on pages 207-208. Stitch the blocks together.

2. Add the sky and ground strips to these blocks.

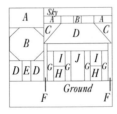

Bear's Paw

Construct the Bear's Paw following the instructions on page 193.

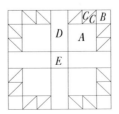

Spools

1. Transfer the corner dots from the pattern (page 248) to the wrong side of A. They are ¼" from the edge so you can use a ruler.

2. Place A and B right sides together. Stitch between the dots on A.

3. Repeat for all four A's, leaving all of the seam allowances free. Do not press yet.

4. Pick up two adjoining A sides and stitch from the center out. Repeat for all four corners.

5. To press: Place the block, wrong side up, on the ironing surface. Press B flat, allowing the other seams to fall into place as you press. Make four blocks.

6. Stitch the blocks together in rows. Join row 1 to row 2.

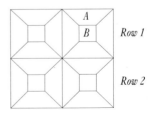

Nine Patch and Hearts

1. Construct two Nine Patch blocks following the instructions on page 41.

2. Stitch a 6½" square to a Nine Patch for rows 1 and 2. Join the rows.

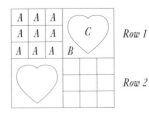

SEWING INSTRUCTIONS FOR DONNA'S SAMPLER

Milky Way

Follow the instructions on page 89 for assembling the Milky Way block.

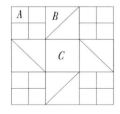

Fans

1. Construct four Fan blocks following the instructions on page 139.

2. Join the blocks into two rows of two blocks each. Join the rows.

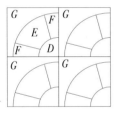

Flying Geese

1. Construct 18 Flying Geese blocks following the instructions on page 73.

2. Join the geese in three vertical rows of six geese in each row. Sew the rows together.

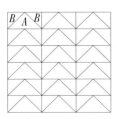

Log Cabin

1. Construct four Log Cabin blocks following the instructions on page 175.

2. Join in the Straight Furrow pattern.

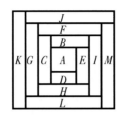

Stars and Hearts

1. Construct five pieced blocks and four Heart blocks following the instructions on page 125.

2. Arrange in rows and stitch row 1 to row 2, and so forth.

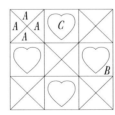

Corner Posts

Stitch two half-square triangles together for the 20 corner posts.

Sashing

Stitch a print strip on each side of the muslin strips.

Quilt Assembly

1. Arrange your blocks in a pleasing manner balancing out the stronger color blocks with the quieter ones. Your arrangement may vary from the one in the photo. You will have three blocks across and four down.

2. Arrange sashing and blocks in rows following quilt drawing on page 243.

3. Stitch blocks and sashes together in rows. Stitch remaining sashes and corner posts in rows. Follow the straight set instructions on page 33 for sewing the blocks together.

4. Follow the instructions on page 33 for adding the borders.

5. Follow the instructions on page 35 for basting the quilt.

6. This quilt is machine-quilted in-the-ditch around all blocks. Machine or hand quilting can be used in the blocks.

7. Follow the instructions on page 37 for binding the quilt.

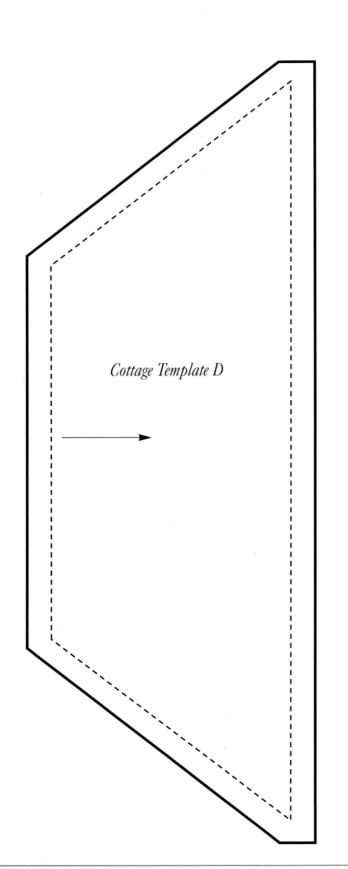

Cottage Template D

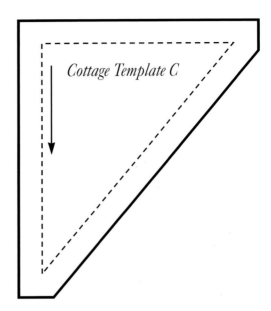

Cottage Template C

Arrows indicate grain line.

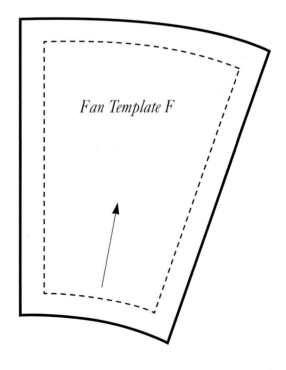

Fan Template F

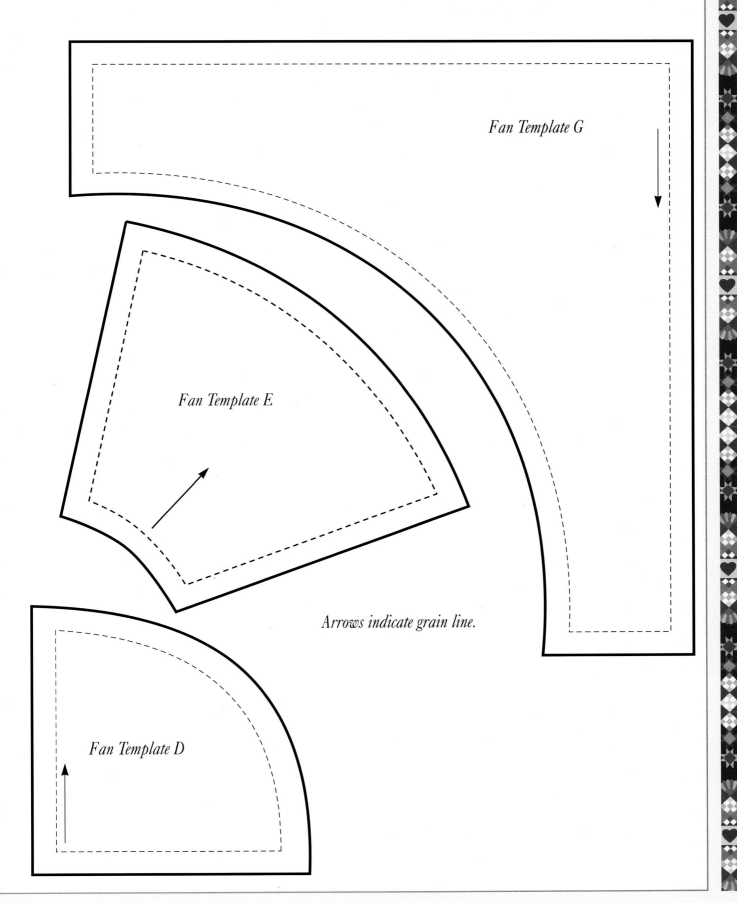

Fan Template G

Fan Template E

Arrows indicate grain line.

Fan Template D

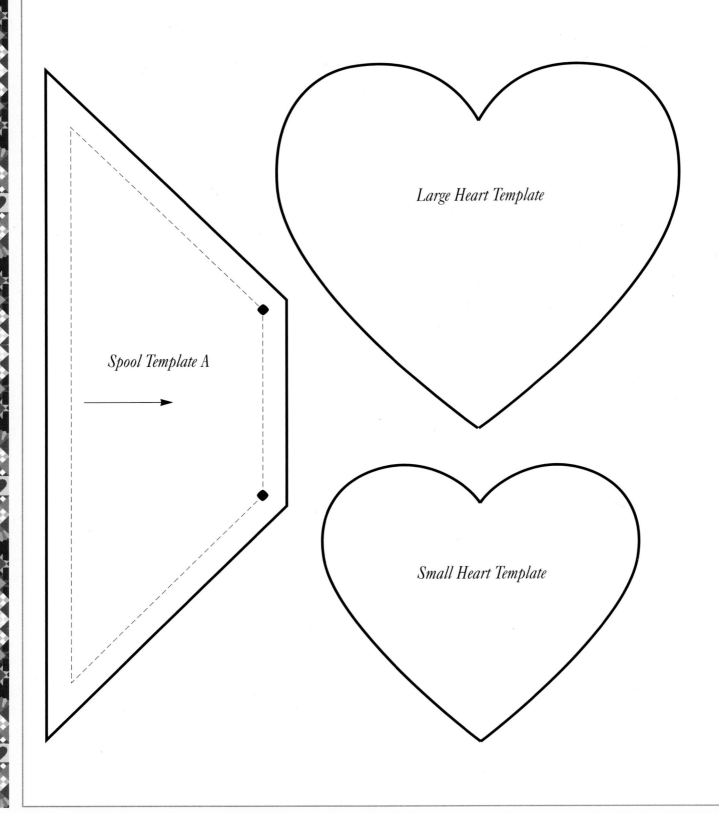

Spool Template A

Large Heart Template

Small Heart Template

GONE FISHING

The finished size is 2½" x 41½".

Refer to quilt drawing and photo for color placement.
You will need to make templates for some patches (page 254).

SUPPLIES

Fish Print
Theme Fabric
¼ yard

Sashing
¼ yard

**Lights, Mediums,
and Darks**
1½ yards total

CUTTING

Theme Fabric: Cut one strip 3½" x 20½".
Checkerboard: Cut two strips 1½" x 42" from each color.
Sashing: Six sashing strips appear between the rows.
All are cut 1½" x 20½" from a dark fabric.

Sawtooth Star (3)
Patch A: Cut three squares 2½" x 2½" for star.
Patch B: Cut 24 squares 1½" x 1½" for star.
Patch C: Cut 12 rectangles 1½" x 2½" for background.
Patch D: Cut 12 squares 1½" x 1½" for background.

House
Patch A: Cut three rectangles 1½" x 2½" for sky.
Patch B: Cut two squares 1½" x 1½" for chimneys.
Patch C: Cut two using House template C (page 234), reversing one, for sky.
Patch D: Cut one using House template D (page 254).
Patch E: Cut one using House template E for roof (page 254).
Patch F: Cut two rectangles 1½" x 4½". Cut one for house side
and one for house front.
Patch G: Cut two rectangles 1¾" x 4" for house.
Patch H: Cut one rectangle 2" x 4" for door.
Patch I: Cut two rectangles 1½" x 2½" for house.
Patch J: Cut one square 2½" x 2½" for window.
Patch K: Cut one rectangle 2" x 4½" for house.

Pine Trees (6)
Patch A: Cut 12 using Pine Tree template A (page 254),
reversing six, for sky.
Patch B: Cut six using Pine Tree template B (page 254) for trees.
Patch C: Cut 12 rectangles 1½" x 1¼" for sky.
Patch D: Cut six rectangles 1½" x 1" for trunks.

Milky Way (4)
Patch A: Cut 16 squares 1½" x 1½" for background.
Patch B: Cut eight background and eight dark squares
1⅞" x 1⅞" for stars. Cut in half diagonally.
Patch C: Cut four dark squares 1½" x 1½" for star centers.
Theme Fabric: Cut one rectangle 3½" x 8½" for inset.

SUPPLIES   # CUTTING

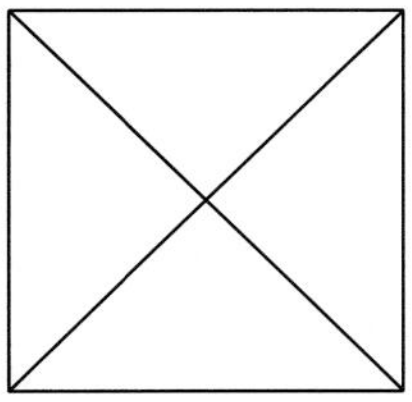

Pieced Blocks (10)
Quarter Squares (10): Cut five squares 3¼" x 3¼" from each of two colors; cut into quarters diagonally.

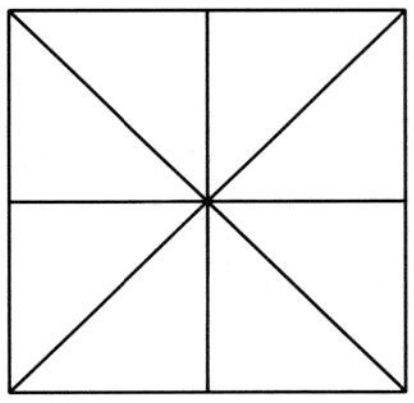

Pinwheels (4)
Pinwheels (4): Cut eight squares 2⅝" x 2⅝" from each of two colors (one light, one dark). Cut in half diagonally.
Corner Triangles: Cut eight squares 3⅜" x 3⅜". Cut in half diagonally.

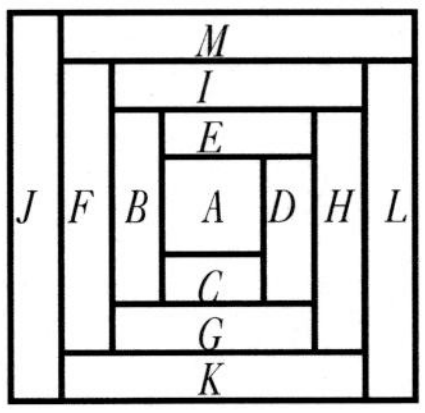

Log Cabin (2)
Patch A (center): Cut two squares 2" x 2".
Logs: All are cut 1¼" wide; lengths are given. Cut two of each.

Light side	Dark side
Patch B: 2"	**Patch D:** 2¾"
Patch C: 2¾"	**Patch E:** 3½"
Patch F: 3½"	**Patch H:** 4¼"
Patch G: 4¼"	**Patch I:** 5"
Patch J: 5"	**Patch L:** 5¾"
Patch K: 5¾"	**Patch M:** 6½"

Theme Fabric: Cut one rectangle 6½" x 8½".

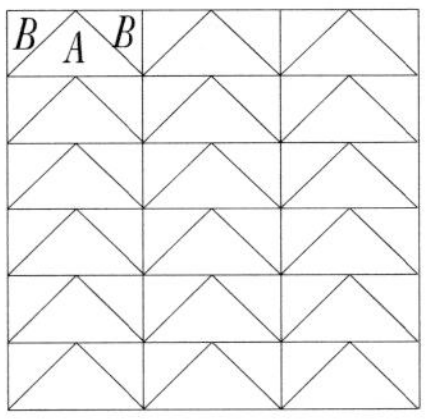

Flying Geese (20)
Patch A: Cut 20 rectangles 1½" x 2½" from dark fabric for geese.
Patch B: Cut 40 squares 1½" x 1½" from light fabric for background.

Border, Binding
½ yard

Border: Cut three strips 2½" x 42". Join into one long strip. From this strip cut two strips 37½" for the sides; cut two strips 24½" for the top and bottom.
Binding: Cut four strips 1¾" x 42". From these strips cut two strips 41½" for the sides; cut two strips 25" for the top and bottom.

Backing
1⅜ yard

Backing: Cut one piece 29" x 46".

Batting 29" x 46"

Sewing instructions begin on next page.

SEWING INSTRUCTIONS FOR GONE FISHING

Review the Quilting Basics in Chapter 2 before you begin.

Instructions are given for individual blocks followed by quilt assembly. You may need to review the construction techniques in individual chapters for each block as you go along.

Checkerboard

Construct a 20"-long Checkerboard strip using the instructions on page 103.

Sawtooth Star

Construct three Stars following the instructions on page 73.

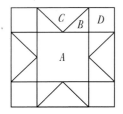

House

Construct the House block following instructions on page 207.

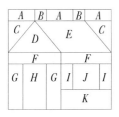

Pine Trees

1. Construct the six Pine Tree blocks following instructions on page 208.

2. Join the blocks into a row.

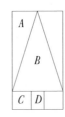

Milky Way

Construct the four Milky Way blocks following the instructions on page 89.

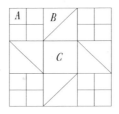

Quarter Squares

1. Construct 10 blocks following the instructions on page 125.

2. Join the blocks into a row.

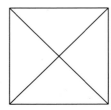

Pinwheels

1. Construct four Pinwheel blocks following the instructions on page 57.

2. Add a setting triangle to each side.

3. Join blocks into a row.

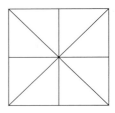

Log Cabin

Construct the two Log Cabin blocks following the instructions on page 175.

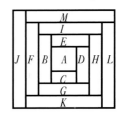

Flying Geese

1. Construct the 20 Flying Geese blocks following the instructions on page 73.

2. Join together so the geese point toward center.

SEWING INSTRUCTIONS FOR GONE FISHING

Quilt Assembly

1. Arrange the blocks according to the quilt drawing. Sew the following blocks into horizontal rows: Stars, Pine Trees, Milky Way, Quarter Squares, Pinwheels, and Flying Geese.

2. Join the Star row to the Pine Tree row. Add the Star/Pine Tree section to the side of the House.

3. Sew Milky Way blocks to each side of the 3½" x 8½" piece of theme fabric.

4. Sew Log Cabin blocks to each side of the 6½" x 8½" piece of theme fabric.

5. Follow the straight set instructions on page 33 for sewing the rows together.

6. Follow the instructions on page 33 for adding the borders.

7. Follow the instructions on page 35 for basting the quilt.

8. This quilt was machine-quilted in-the-ditch.

9. Follow the instructions on page 37 for binding the quilt.

Gone Fishing Quilt Drawing

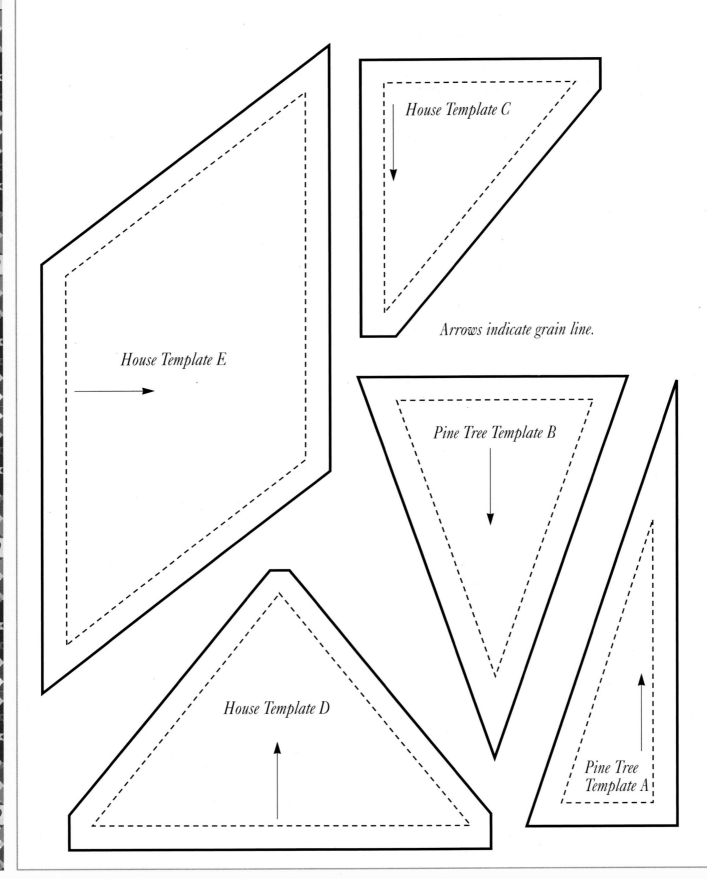

House Template C

Arrows indicate grain line.

House Template E

Pine Tree Template B

House Template D

Pine Tree
Template A

ACKNOWLEDGMENTS

Patchwork Quilts Made Easy is a publication that could not have happened without a dedicated editorial staff. Suzanne Nelson, Ellen Pahl, and Karen Soltys of Rodale Press lent ideas as well as copyediting skills. Thank you to Barb Kuhn and Louise Townsend for their fine tuning of the charts on the computer and their copy editing. Dalene Stone did the project checking for which I am most grateful.

Without Liz Aneloski's organizational skills, hard work, and attention to detail, this book would not have been a reality. Thank you, Liz. And my sincere appreciation to Todd and Tony Hensley, the owners of C&T Publishing, for believing in my ideas and committing to them.

The following quilting friends were invaluable as they helped me to stitch, quilt, and plan the 49 quilts for this book. My heartfelt thank you to Ursula Searles, Lawry Thorn, Cathi Howell, Joanne Myers, Andrea Balosky, Rhondi Hindman, Marrell Dickson, Carrol Clark, Diane Rupp, Julie Hensley, Jackie Erickson, Barbara Slater, Nancy Gray, Sherie Baldner, Sandi Abernathy, Victoria Brady, Liz Aneloski, Ruth Ingham, and Jean Humenansky.

Pictures are such a valuable learning tool as well as inspiration in any publication. My photographer Ross Chandler and I have worked on many projects, and his creative eye is as valuable as his technical skill. Diane Pederson and Liz Aneloski came to Sisters, and we spent three days loading and unloading the cars, setting up shots, waiting for the perfect light. My thanks to them.

Sisters is a very special place to live and work. My fellow business associates either lent me props or let me photograph in their front yards. Through these photos the essence of Sisters is captured. My sincere thanks goes to Ponderosa Properties, Wonser Gallery, Mountain Man Trading, Ponderosa Woodworking, Conklin's Bed and Breakfast, Sisters Floral, Timeless Treasures, Ray and Pat April, Sisters Drug, Designs Unlimited, and Good Family Magazines.

The doll on page 87 was made by Barbara Willis who has her own pattern company.

Dennis McGregor painted all of the beautiful quilt block designs for the book as well as lent his garden and garden shed for photographs.

My family is so understanding when I am on a deadline, and they always lend moral support as well as technical skills. Thank you, Jason, for all the help with formatting on the computer; Valori, thank you for your encouragement, inspiration, and use of your wonderful shelves of herbs and dried flowers; and John, thank you for your never-ending faith in me and believing that I can finish on time.

OTHER FINE QUILTING BOOKS FROM C&T PUBLISHING

By Jean Wells:

A Celebration of Hearts
With Marina Anderson

Memorabilia Quilting

NSA Series:
Bloomin' Creations
Holiday Magic
Hometown
Fans, Hearts, & Folk Art

Picture This
With Marina Anderson

PQME Series:
Basket Quilt
Bear's Paw Quilt
Country Bunny Quilt
Milky Way Quilt
Nine-Patch Quilt
Pinwheel Quilt
Sawtooth Star Quilt
Stars & Hearts Quilt

And By Others:

An Amish Adventure
Roberta Horton

Appliqué 12 Easy Ways!
Elly Sienkiewicz

Appliqué 12 Borders and Medallions!
Elly Sienkiewicz

The Art of Silk Ribbon Embroidery
Judith Baker Montano

Baltimore Album Quilts,
Historic Notes and Antique Patterns
Elly Sienkiewicz

Baltimore Album Revival!
Historic Quilts in the Making.
The Catalog of C&T Publishing's
Quilt Show and Contest
Elly Sienkiewicz

Baltimore Beauties and Beyond,
Volume I
Elly Sienkiewicz

Baltimore Beauties and Beyond,
Volume II
Elly Sienkiewicz

The Best From Gooseberry Hill:
Patterns For Stuffed Animals & Dolls
Kathy Pace

Christmas Traditions From the Heart
Margaret Peters

Christmas Traditions From the Heart,
Volume Two
Margaret Peters

A Colorful Book
Yvonne Porcella

Colors Changing Hue
Yvonne Porcella

Crazy Quilt Handbook
Judith Montano

Crazy Quilt Odyssey
Judith Montano

Design a Baltimore Album Quilt!
Elly Sienkiewicz

Dimensional Appliqué—
Baskets, Blooms & Baltimore Borders
Elly Sienkiewicz

Elegant Stitches
Judith Baker Montano

Fantastic Figures: Ideas & Techniques
Using the New Clays
Susanna Oroyan

14,287 Pieces of Fabrics and Other Poems
Jean Ray Laury

Friendship's Offering
Susan McKelvey

Happy Trails
Pepper Cory

Heirloom Machine Quilting
Harriet Hargrave

Imagery on Fabric
Jean Ray Laury

Isometric Perspective
Katie Pasquini-Masopust

Landscapes & Illusions
Joen Wolfrom

The Magical Effects of Color
Joen Wolfrom

Mariner's Compass
Judy Mathieson

Mastering Machine Appliqué
Harriet Hargrave

The New Lone Star Handbook
Blanche Young and Helen Young Frost

Pattern Play
Doreen Speckmann

Perfect Pineapples
Jane Hall and Dixie Haywood

Pieced Clothing
Yvonne Porcella

Pieced Clothing Variations
Yvonne Porcella

Quilts for Fabric Lovers
Alex Anderson

Quilts, Quilts, and More Quilts!
Diana McClun and Laura Nownes

Recollections
Judith Baker Montano

Stitching Free: Easy Machine Pictures
Shirley Nilsson

Symmetry: A Design System for
Quiltmakers
Ruth B. McDowell

3 Dimensional Design
Katie Pasquini

A Treasury of Quilt Labels
Susan McKelvey

Virginia Avery's Hats
A Heady Affair

Virginia Avery's Nifty Neckwear

Visions: Quilts, Layers of Excellence
Quilt San Diego

Whimsical Animals
Miriam Gourley

For more information write for a free catalog from:

C&T Publishing
P.O. Box 1456
Lafayette, CA 94549
(1-800-284-1114)